D0310421

Eaton's Modern Ready Reckoner

535

EATON'S

MODERN *READY* RECKONER

A 21ST-CENTURY GUIDE TO

BITCOIN   MEGACITIES

MONARCHS

EMOJIS   TWITTER

ETC.

Published by 535
An imprint of Blink Publishing
2.25, The Plaza,
535 Kings Road,
Chelsea Harbour,
London, SW10 0SZ

www.blinkpublishing.co.uk

facebook.com/blinkpublishing
twitter.com/blinkpublishing

Hardback – 978-1-7887-0082-5
Ebook – 978-1-7887-0083-2

A CIP catalogue of this book is available from the British Library.

Printed and bound by Clays Ltd, Elcograf S.p.A

3 5 7 9 10 8 6 4 2

Blink Publishing is an imprint of Bonnier Books UK
www.bonnierbooks.co.uk

I dedicate the book, with love and gratitude, to my family:
Jo, Alexander and Matilda, who was born while I was writing it.

"Curiosity is one of the permanent and certain characteristics
of a vigorous intellect"

Dr Samuel Johnson, *The Rambler* (1751)

"Curiosity killed the cat"

Proverb

INTRODUCTION

What, you may ask, is a ready reckoner? The *Oxford English Dictionary* defines it as "a book or table listing for ready reference the results of standard numerical calculations". The first one was published in 1757 by the grammarian Daniel Fenning and its subtitle – "trade's most useful assistant" – indicates the intended readership. The original ready reckoners were practical handbooks for practical people: builders, craftsmen, shopkeepers and bookkeepers. Even hangmen used them to calculate the right rope length for the weight of the person to be executed. They were a handy source of accurate information in an age long before the pocket calculator, never mind the advent of the Internet. To our modern eyes the old ready reckoners can seem archaic, but they were treasure troves of information. Was there really a time when it was "very necessary to be known in business" that a load of Scots coals was one hundredweight or that a wey of Suffolk cheese equalled 42 cloves (336 lbs)?

This book revives the idea of the ready reckoner as an old-fashioned antidote to the information overload of the digital age. It is an eclectic anthology of modern general knowledge, sometimes trivial but always informative. There is a smattering of history, but the focus is on today's world. The subjects range from activism to art theft, bitcoin to bizarre books, Twitter to Trump and tattoos. To give a flavour of the old ready reckoners, there are some traditional weights and measures conversions, a table of dates and even a guide to calculating the height of a tree.

As a child I immersed myself in encyclopedias and reference books. Most of my working life has been spent devising quizzes for TV and newspapers. My aim with this book was simple: write something that I'd enjoy dipping into myself. So, if the Wi-Fi is down, or you just fancy switching off your smartphone, dive in!

Finally, I would like to thank my editor, Joel Simons, who approached me with the idea of the modern ready reckoner you now hold in your hands, as well as everyone at 535 and Blink Publishing.

Thomas Eaton
Cricklewood, 2018

─────────────── **MUSEUMS OF CURIOSITY** ───────────────

Unusual collections from around the world.

British Lawnmower Museum in Southport, Merseyside. Includes the world's first solar-powered robotic lawnmower and a genuine mower that measures only 2 inches long.

Cup Noodles Museum in Osaka, Japan. Celebrates the invention of instant noodles in 1958 by Momofuku Ando. They were chicken flavoured. He later pioneered cup noodles and even noodles designed to be eaten in space.

Derwent Pencil Museum in Keswick, Cumbria. Based in the Lake District home of the first pencil. Highlights include wartime pencils with hidden maps and one of the world's largest pencils at almost 8m long.

Dog Collar Museum at Leeds Castle in Kent. More than 130 examples of canine neckwear, dating from the 15th century to the present day.

Don Quixote Iconographic Museum in Guanajuato, Mexico. A museum in which every exhibit is an artistic representation of Cervantes' hero Don Quixote.

Esperanto Museum in Vienna, Austria. Dedicated to the artificial language created in the late 19th century by the Polish ophthalmologist L.L. Zamenhof. He believed a new international language would enhance the prospect of world peace.

Frietmuseum in Bruges, Belgium. The world's only museum dedicated to the humble potato chip.

Icelandic Phallological Museum in Reykjavík. Contains penis specimens from almost all the land and sea mammals found in Iceland, including whales, seals, walruses and one very angry polar bear. Humans, too.

International Cryptozoology Museum in Portland, Maine. Collections relating to animals as yet unknown to science, including "genuine" Yeti hair samples and faecal matter.

Kansas Barbed Wire Museum in La Crosse, Kansas. Patented by Joseph Glidden in 1874, barbed wire was a surprisingly effective weapon in taming the Wild West. Land was divided up and bison, cattle and cowboys never roamed as free again.

Leila's Hair Museum in Independence, Missouri. Over 600 wreaths and more than 2,000 pieces of jewellery, all made from human hair.

Meguro Parasitological Museum in Tokyo, Japan. Its star exhibit is an 8.8m tapeworm.

Museum of Broken Relationships in Los Angeles and Zagreb, Croatia. It illustrates failed relationships through a display of personal objects left by ex-lovers.

Museum of Failure in Helsingborg, Sweden. Dedicated to products that never caught on, it includes the Sony Betamax, Google Glass, Bic for Her and Harley-Davidson perfume.

Sulabh International Museum of Toilets in New Delhi, India. The history of toilets and sanitation from the third millennium BC to the end of the 20th century.

—————— COUNTING AND COUNTERING THE CALORIES ——————

These are the calories burned by a 75kg person undertaking a variety of activities for an hour at a time.

Running at 8mph .... 1,013 kcals	Golf 338
Swimming fast front crawl 825	Gardening 300
Competitive football 750	Walking moderately 300
Running at 6mph 750	Vacuuming 263
Step aerobics 638	Birdwatching 188
Dancing 488	Ironing 173
Walking briskly 338	Typing at a computer 75

———— GOOGLE RULES THE WORLD (ALMOST) ————

Worldwide search engine and browser market share, 2018.

GOOGLE .... 91.25% — No surprises here. It began life in 1996 at Stanford University where Sergey Brin and Larry Page developed a search algorithm called BackRub.

BING .... 3.08% — Microsoft's challenger, launched in 2009.

YAHOO! .... 2.13% — Japan remains stubbornly loyal to Yahoo!, and it retains a 25% share there.

BAIDU .... 1.48% — In China, Baidu has between 70–80% of the market share.

YANDEX .... 0.68% — Yandex is the market leader in Russia and most of the countries in the former Soviet Union.

DUCKDUCKGO .... 0.25% — Launched in 2008 and named after a children's game; it aims to protect searchers' privacy and blocks advertising trackers.

CHROME .... 57.69% — Google's freeware browser, launched in 2008. It took under four years for Chrome to overtake Microsoft's Internet Explorer as the world's most used browser.

SAFARI .... 14.79% — At its launch in 2003 Steve Jobs said, with characteristic modesty, "we predict that many will feel it is the best browser ever created".

It has enjoyed a steady market share ever since as the default browser on Apple products.

UC BROWSER .... 7.35% — Chinese browser, developed by UCWeb, part of the Internet giant Alibaba Group.

FIREFOX .... 5.4% — Launched by Mozilla in 2002. It is the most popular browser in Cuba.

OPERA .... 3.65% — Developed in Norway and released in 1997.

INTERNET
EXPLORER .... 3.13% — Its decline has been precipitous; in 2003 it enjoyed a 95% market share. In 2016, Microsoft ended support for all but the latest version of IE.

HOMEPAGE DOODLING

The Google search page is many people's first stop on the Internet. And the doodle, a topical alteration of the Google logo, has become a familiar part of the online landscape. Created in 1998, the first doodle was intended as a cryptic out-of-office message. Company founders Larry Page and Sergey Brin were away at the Burning Man festival in Nevada and they put a stick figure (a symbol of the festival) behind the second "o" of Google.

The doodle really got going two years later when intern (now webmaster) Dennis Hwang designed an image for Bastille Day. It was an instant hit and he was appointed Google's chief doodler. Since then, illustrators and engineers have devised over 2,000 doodles for Google's homepages across the world. The first animated doodle in 2010 celebrated Isaac Newton's birthday, showing an apple falling from a tree. Later that year the first interactive doodle was a playable version of Pac-Man, created to mark the game's 40th anniversary.

PERSONALITY TEST

Of the many attempts to analyse human personality, one of the more successful was the inventory of 16 types devised in the mid-20th century by Katharine Cook Briggs and her daughter Isabel Briggs Myers. These are combined below with the model of four temperaments developed by David Keirsey.

GUARDIANS

Inspector .... (Introverted, Sensing, Thinking, Judging)
Protector .... (Introverted, Sensing, Feeling, Judging)
Provider .... (Extroverted, Sensing, Feeling, Judging)
Supervisor .... (Extroverted, Sensing, Thinking, Judging)

ARTISANS

Composer .... (Introverted, Sensing, Feeling, Perceiving)
Crafter .... (Introverted, Sensing, Thinking, Perceiving)
Promoter .... (Extroverted, Sensing, Thinking, Perceiving)
Performer .... (Extroverted, Sensing, Feeling, Perceiving)

IDEALISTS

Teacher .... (Extroverted, Intuitive, Feeling, Judging)
Champion .... (Extroverted, Intuitive, Feeling, Perceiving)
Healer .... (Introverted, Intuitive, Feeling, Perceiving)
Counsellor .... (Introverted, Intuitive, Feeling, Judging)

RATIONALS

Inventor .... (Extroverted, Intuitive, Thinking, Perceiving)
Mastermind .... (Introverted, Intuitive, Thinking, Judging)
Field Marshal .... (Extroverted, Intuitive, Thinking, Judging)
Architect .... (Introverted, Intuitive, Thinking, Perceiving)

———— TITANS OF TOYS ————

Winners of "Toy of the Year" for each year of this decade so far, awarded by the Toy Retailers Association.

L.O.L. Surprise, 2017. Collectable dolls with mix and match accessories.

Hatchimals, 2016. Robotic creatures that hatch themselves from an egg.

Pie Face, 2015. Game of jeopardy, usually ending up in a splatted face.

Snow Glow Elsa doll, 2014. From the Disney film *Frozen*.

Teksta Robotic Puppy, 2013. Responds to voice, movement, lights and sounds.

Furby, 2012. Revival of a classic, now with LCD eyes and a mobile app.

LeapPad Explorer, 2011. Simple tablet computer, for games and learning.

Jet Pack Buzz Lightyear, 2010. To infinity and beyond!

———— OIL: THE CRUDE FACTS ————

As recently as 2014, BP predicted that the world's oil would only last another 53 years. With new oil finds and the growth of hydraulic fracking and shale oil, the picture has changed. Within the next decade the US could become a net oil exporter for the first time since the 1950s. These are the proven oil reserves of the major producers.

Country	Reserves (billions of barrels)	Country	Reserves (billions of barrels)
Venezuela	301	Kuwait	102
Saudi Arabia	266	UAE	98
Canada	170	Russia	80
Iran	158	Libya	48
Iraq	143	USA	35

QUAKING IN OUR BOOTS

There is more than one way to measure an earthquake. The Richter magnitude scale is based on the energy released by an earthquake, measured using a seismograph. The Mercalli intensity scale, on the other hand, describes the surface effects of the quake and relies on observation.

Richter scale	Mercalli scale	Experienced by observers
1–2	I	Felt by few people; barely noticeable
2–3	II	Felt by a few people, especially on upper floors
3–4	III	Noticeable indoors, especially on upper floors
4	IV	Felt by many indoors; few outdoors
4–5	V	Felt by almost everyone; some people woken up. Small objects moved; trees and poles may shake
5–6	VI	Felt by everyone; difficult to stand; some heavy furniture is moved; some plaster falls
6	VII	Well-built structures may have slight to moderate damage; poorly built structures may be badly damaged; walls may collapse
6–7	VIII	Little damage in specially-built buildings; major damage to ordinary buildings; severe damage to poorly built structures
7	IX	Buildings moved off foundations; large cracks in the ground, large scale destruction; landslides
7–8	X	Destruction of most buildings; severe ground cracking; landslides; large-scale destruction
8	XI	Total damage; few buildings left standing; bridges destroyed; waves seen on the ground
8+	XII	Total damage; waves seen on the ground; objects thrown up in the air

The largest earthquake ever recorded, measuring 9.5 on the Richter scale, took place in 1960 in Valdivia, Chile.

PUTTING A NEW YOU TOGETHER

The development of human organ transplants, piece by piece.

Skin, 1869 – first skin graft performed by Jacques-Louis Reverdin.

Cornea, 1905 – first cornea transplant took place in Moravia. Uniquely, the cornea doesn't need a blood supply to survive so it can be used for transplants up to 24 hours after death.

Kidney, 1954 – first successful kidney transplant performed in Boston. A living donor gave a kidney to his identical twin.

Lung, 1963 – first lung transplant, at the University of Mississippi. The patient died two weeks later and it would be another 20 years before a long-term success was achieved. The procedure is complicated by the fact that lung tissue deteriorates very quickly away from the human body.

Liver, 1967 – first successful liver transplant. Performed by Thomas Starzl in Denver. He had carried out the same procedure four years earlier, but the organ was rejected by the recipient's body.

Heart, 1967 – first heart transplant. Performed in Cape Town, South Africa by Dr Christiaan Barnard. The patient Louis Washkansky survived for 18 days before succumbing to pneumonia.

Heart and lung, 1981 – first successful combined heart-lung transplant carried out at Stanford Hospital, California.

Hand, 1999 – successfully carried out on Matthew Scott in Kentucky. The procedure had been carried out in France in 1998 but within three years the patient requested that his new "Frankenstein" limb be amputated.

Face, 2010 – first successful full-face transplant, done in Barcelona. The patient, the victim of a shooting accident, received new cheekbones, facial muscles, jaw, palate, lips and nose.

Penis, 2015 – the recipient was a South African man who had suffered from the complications of a botched adult circumcision.

---------------------- **FIRST TWEETS ON TWITTER** ----------------------

The first ever Twitter message was posted in 2006 by its co-founder Jack Dorsey: *just setting up my twttr.*

President Obama was an early adopter of the platform. His first tweet in 2007 proved to be tragically optimistic: *Thinking we're only one signature away from ending the war in Iraq.*

When the CIA joined Twitter in 2014, its first message showed a sense of humour: *We can neither confirm nor deny that this is our first tweet.*

Britain's intelligence agency GCHQ tweeted for the first time in 2016, with a message hinting at its role in global surveillance: *Hello, world.*

But Twitter really belongs to its celebrity tweeters and few are more prolific than Kim Kardashian, who joined in 2009: *Hey guys it's Kim Kardashian! I finally signed up for Twitter! There are a few fakes so just know this is the real me!!!*

A month earlier the singer Katy Perry had tweeted for the first time: *Just got into Berlin... feeling better thank you, have my vicks inhaler by my bedside... and P.S. I TWITTTTER! GAH. Such a follower!* She is now the most-followed person on Twitter, with over 107 million people reading her messages.

Even the Vatican got involved and in 2012 Pope Benedict XVI began tweeting using the handle @pontifex: *Dear friends, I am pleased to get in touch with you through Twitter. Thank you for your generous response. I bless all of you from my heart.*

The Queen tweeted for the first time in 2014: *It is a pleasure to open the Information Age exhibition today at the @ScienceMuseum and I hope people will enjoy visiting. Elizabeth R.*

Britain's most improbable Twitter celebrity is the former Labour MP Ed Balls. In 2011, while Shadow Chancellor, he tweeted his own name by accident and the anniversary of that message, 28 April, is now "celebrated" on Twitter as Ed Balls Day.

AND HERE IS THE FAKE NEWS

"Fake news" was the *Collins Dictionary* word of the year in 2017, defined as "false, often sensational, information disseminated under the guise of news reporting". Lies and propaganda are nothing new, of course, but in the age of social media untruths can travel around the world at the click of a button. Here are some of the most insidious, and most ridiculous, recent examples of fake news (most, it appears, involving Donald Trump).

Barack Obama was not born in the USA and is a secret Muslim.

A Gay Girl in Damascus blog (purported to be a girl's experience of the civil war in Syria but later exposed as the work of an American man).

Leading Democrat politicians operated a child sex ring based at the Washington pizza restaurant Comet Ping Pong.

People at a Donald Trump rally in Manhattan chanted "We hate Muslims, we hate blacks, we want our great country back".

Melania Trump employs a body double for official functions.

In the Donbass conflict, Ukrainian soldiers crucified an ethnic Russian boy.

The crowd at Glastonbury cheered Radiohead tuning their instruments, thinking it was a song.

German Chancellor Merkel's hair was pixelated when she appeared on Saudi Arabian state television.

The Palestinian National Authority recognised Texas as part of Mexico in retaliation for President Trump's acceptance of Jerusalem as the Israeli capital.

Donald Trump's presidential inauguration was the best-attended ever (they had the doctored photos to prove it).

Trump ordered the execution of Thanksgiving turkeys pardoned by President Obama.

In 2018, FEMA (Federal Emergency Management Agency) used two barges to take people fleeing a Hawaiian volcano eruption to an "internment camp".

Mount Rushmore was defaced in 2018 with graffiti reading "Obama was here" and "Fuck Trump".

THE TSAR WITH THE DRAGON TATTOO

Getting ink done has never been more popular. These are some surprising tattoo owners and body art enthusiasts.

King George V – in 1881, while serving with the Royal Navy, the future monarch was tattooed in Japan. While it was never publicly displayed, it's thought to have been a red and blue dragon on his arm.

Nicholas II – ten years later, also in Japan, George V's cousin, the future Russian Tsar, got a tattoo: a dragon on his right arm.

Winston Churchill – the prime minister had an anchor tattooed on his forearm. It's widely reported that his mother Jennie had a snake design on her wrist, but photographic evidence appears to contradict this.

Sean Connery – "Scotland forever" and "Mum and Dad" on his right arm.

The Enigma – the US sideshow performer Paul Lawrence has a jigsaw puzzle design tattooed over his entire body.

David Beckham – he got his first tattoo in 1999, a tribute to his son Brooklyn on his back, followed by his wife Victoria's name in Hindi on his arm. Over 40 tattoos later a solar system design was added in 2018 on his scalp, suggesting he's running out of skin to ink.

Miley Cyrus – she has over 40 tattoos, including a tribute to her dog Floyd, who was killed by a coyote.

Ed Sheeran – the singer has over 60 tattoos, including a Heinz ketchup label, a Henri Matisse sketch and a teddy bear. Perhaps his most celebrated inking is a large tiger head in the middle of his chest.

Judi Dench – for her 81st birthday in 2016, she had the Latin motto "carpe diem" (seize the day) tattooed on her wrist.

Vivien Bodycote – as a Valentine's Day present in 2018, the 60-year-old grandmother from Leicestershire had her 35th tattoo of football manager José Mourinho.

Justin Bieber – in 2017 he revealed a full-torso tattoo of gothic images that had taken 26 hours to complete.

—————— PEOPLE IN GREENHOUSES... ——————

The greenhouse effect is caused by gases absorbing heat energy from the Earth's surface and radiating it back. With the heat unable to escape into space, the result is global warming and climate change. These so-called greenhouse gases are the chief culprits.

Water vapour – the most abundant greenhouse gas in the atmosphere, although its concentration is a result of climate "feedback" rather than human activity. The warmer the Earth's surface, the greater the evaporation of water, which builds up in the lower atmosphere as vapour. This concentration of water vapour absorbs more heat radiated from the Earth, warming the atmosphere even further. Thus, it amplifies the climatic effects of the other gases.

Carbon dioxide – the most important greenhouse gas. It enters the atmosphere through the burning of fossil fuels (oil, coal and gas), trees and wood and as a result of industrial processes, such as cement making. In 2017, an estimated 41 billion metric tons of carbon dioxide was produced globally, accounting for around 76% of all anthropogenic (man-made) greenhouse gas emissions. It's not all bad news, though, as carbon dioxide is removed from the atmosphere when it is absorbed by plants as part of photosynthesis.

Methane – less prevalent than carbon dioxide (16% of global emissions) but more potent. It remains in the atmosphere for less time, around a decade, rather than hundreds of years as in the case of carbon dioxide. Farting cows are a major source of methane, as are wetlands, rice cultivation and the decay of organic matter in landfill sites.

Ozone – low-level ozone, caused by air pollution, is a greenhouse gas.

Nitrous oxide and fluorinated gases – produced by industrial activities, the latter group includes hydrofluorocarbons (HFCs) and perfluorocarbons (PFCs).

———————— LONG TO REIGN OVER US ————————

"There will soon be only five kings left: the kings of England, diamonds, hearts, spades and clubs" – King Farouk of Egypt (deposed in 1952).

These are the world's remaining monarchies.

UK AND EUROPE

United Kingdom and the Commonwealth – Queen Elizabeth II ascended the British throne in 1952.

Spain – Juan Carlos I ruled until 2014 when he abdicated in favour of his son Felipe VI.

Sweden – Carl XVI Gustaf, king since 1973.

Norway – Harald V, king since 1991.

The Netherlands – Willem-Alexander became king in 2013 on the abdication of his mother Queen Beatrix.

Belgium – Philippe, king of the Belgians since 2013.

Luxembourg – Henri, grand duke since 2000. He is a first cousin of Philippe of Belgium.

Liechtenstein – Prince Hans-Adam II, since 1989.

Andorra – in a unique constitutional arrangement, Andorra has joint heads of state known as co-princes. They are the President of France and the Bishop of Urgell, currently Emmanuel Macron and Joan-Enric Vives i Sicília.

Monaco – Prince Albert II, since 2005. He competed for Monaco in the bobsleigh at five consecutive Winter Olympics.

The Vatican – Pope Francis, since 2013.

THE MIDDLE EAST

Saudi Arabia – Salman, king since 2015.

Kuwait – Sabah Al-Ahmad Al-Jaber Al-Sabah, emir since 2006.

Qatar – Tamim bin Hamad Al Thani, emir since 2013.

United Arab Emirates – the UAE is a federation of seven emirates, ruled by six royal houses.

Bahrain – Hamad bin Isa bin Salman Al Khalifa became emir in 1999 and declared himself the first King of Bahrain in 2002.

Jordan – Abdullah II, king since 1999. He is considered to be a 41st generation direct descendant of the Prophet Muhammad.

Oman – Qaboos bin Said Al Said, sultan since 1970.

AFRICA

Morocco – Mohammed VI, king since 1999.

Swaziland – Mswati III, king since 1986. He has fifteen wives, at the last count. The Queen Mother of Swaziland has the title Ndlovukati, literally meaning She-Elephant.

Lesotho – Letsie III, king since 1996.

ASIA

Japan – Akihito, emperor since 1989. The world's last remaining emperor, he is the 125th member in a line of rulers stretching back to the 7th century BC.

Thailand – Maha Vajiralongkorn Bodindradebayavarangkun (or Rama X), king since 2016. Having reigned for over 70 years, his father Bhumibol Adulyadej was the world's longest-serving head of state.

Brunei – Hassanal Bolkiah, sultan since 1967.

Cambodia – Norodom Sihamoni, king since 2004. The Cambodian monarchy was restored in 1993 on an elective basis.

Malaysia – uniquely, Malaysia has a "revolving" monarchy; the country's nine hereditary state rulers take turns as the country's king for five-year terms. Since 2016, the ruler has been Sultan Muhammad V.

Bhutan – since 2006 Jigme Khesar Namgyel Wangchuck has been the Druk Gyalpo (or Dragon King) of this Himalayan kingdom.

Tonga – Tupou VI ascended the Tongan throne in 2012. It is the only indigenous monarchy in the Pacific.

—————— **KIND HEARTS AND CORONETS** ——————

On being shown a chart of the line of succession in 1830, the future Queen Victoria simply said "I will be good". This is the House of Windsor's revised line of succession after the birth of Prince Louis on St George's Day, 2018. The first six people in the list need to ask the Queen's permission to marry.

1 .... Charles, Prince of Wales
2 .... Prince William, Duke of Cambridge
3 .... Prince George
4 .... Princess Charlotte
5 .... Prince Louis
6 .... Prince Henry (Harry), Duke of Sussex
7 .... Prince Andrew, Duke of York
8 .... Princess Beatrice
9 .... Princess Eugenie
10 .... Prince Edward, Earl of Wessex

—————— **GOING ROUND IN CIRCLES 1** ——————

The countries you pass through while travelling along some of the Earth's imaginary lines.

Greenwich Meridian (North to South)
UK • France • Spain • Algeria • Mali • Burkina Faso • Togo • Ghana • Antarctica

---------------- **GREENWICH MEANS TIME** ----------------

GMT is the mean solar time at the 0° longitude of the Royal Observatory in Greenwich. The world sets its clocks to this time, now known internationally as Coordinated Universal Time (UTC). These are the time adjustments in hours (and occasionally half hours) made across the globe.

-10 .... Honolulu
-9 .... Anchorage
-8 .... Los Angeles, San Francisco, Seattle, Tijuana, Vancouver
-7 .... Calgary, Phoenix
-6 .... Chicago, Mexico City, San José, San Salvador, Winnipeg
-5 .... Bogota, Havana, Kingston, Lima, New York, Toronto
-4 .... Caracas, Halifax, La Paz, Manaus, Port of Spain, Santiago
-3 .... Buenos Aires, Montevideo, Rio de Janeiro
-2 .... South Georgia and the South Sandwich Islands
-1 .... Azores, Cape Verde, Greenland
0 .... Accra, Casablanca, Dublin, Lisbon, London, Reykjavík
+1 .... Amsterdam, Berlin, Brussels, Madrid, Paris, Rome
+2 .... Athens, Bucharest, Cairo, Helsinki, Jerusalem, Kiev
+3 .... Baghdad, Istanbul, Moscow, Nairobi, Baghdad, Doha,
+3.30 .... Tehran
+4 .... Baku, Dubai, Samara, Yerevan, Tbilisi
+4.30 .... Kabul
+5 .... Astana, Ashgabat, Karachi, Tashkent, Yekaterinburg
+5.30 .... Delhi, Colombo, Kolkata, Mumbai
+5.45 .... Kathmandu
+6 .... Bishkek, Dhaka, Omsk
+6.30 .... Rangoon
+7 .... Bangkok, Jakarta, Ho Chi Minh City, Novosibirsk
+8 .... Beijing, Kuala Lumpur, Manila, Perth, Singapore
+9 .... Pyongyang, Seoul, Tokyo
+9.30 .... Adelaide
+10 .... Port Moresby, Sydney, Vladivostok
+11 .... Vanuatu
+12 .... Auckland, Fiji
+13 .... Samoa
+14 .... Kiribati (Line Islands)

──── HERITAGE SOS ────

**UNESCO-designated world heritage sites in the UK
and in British Overseas Territories.**

ENGLAND

Blenheim Palace

Canterbury Cathedral,
    St Augustine's Abbey and
    St Martin's Church

City of Bath

Cornwall and West Devon
    Mining Landscape

Derwent Valley Mills

Dorset and East Devon Coast

Durham Castle and Cathedral

Frontiers of the Roman Empire
    (Hadrian's Wall)

Ironbridge Gorge

Lake District

Liverpool – Maritime Mercantile
    City

Maritime Greenwich

Palace of Westminster and
    Westminster Abbey

Royal Botanic Gardens, Kew

Saltaire (Victorian model village)

Stonehenge, Avebury and
    associated sites

Studley Royal Park including the
    Ruins of Fountains Abbey

Tower of London

Liverpool has been placed on
    the "in danger" list
    because its historic waterfront
    is deemed to be under threat
    from development schemes.

SCOTLAND

Forth Bridge

Frontiers of the Roman Empire
    (Antonine Wall)

Neolithic Orkney

New Lanark

Old and New Towns of
    Edinburgh

St Kilda
    (archipelago including the
    westernmost of the Hebrides)

WALES

Blaenavon Industrial Landscape

Castles and Town Walls of
    King Edward in Gwynedd

Pontcysyllte Aqueduct
    and Canal

NORTHERN IRELAND

Giant's Causeway and
    Causeway Coast

OVERSEAS TERRITORIES

Gorham's Cave Complex
(Gibraltar)
Gough and Inaccessible Islands
(South Atlantic)
Henderson Island

(Pitcairn Islands,
South Pacific)
Historic Town of St George
and Related Fortifications
(Bermuda)

STATES IN STASIS

Disputed polities that are struggling for international recognition.

Abkhazia – part of the former Soviet Union, it declared independence from Georgia in the 1990s after civil and ethnic unrest. Russia recognised the state in 2008 following its own conflict with Georgia.

Kosovo – part of the former Yugoslavia and still claimed by Serbia. It declared independence in 2008 and is recognised by over 100 UN members.

Northern Cyprus – recognised only by Turkey, which invaded Cyprus in 1974 leading to the division of the island.

South Ossetia – another restive part of Georgia that broke away in the 1990s and retains close links to Russia.

Republic of China – usually known as Taiwan, or Chinese Taipei when it competes at the Olympics. The People's Republic of China claims jurisdiction over Taiwan as part of its one-China policy.

Sahrawi Republic – a strip of land in the Western Sahara proclaimed in 1976 by the Polisario Front, a liberation movement aiming to end Moroccan presence there. Morocco claims the territory.

Transnistria – the Pridnestrovian Moldavian Republic, to give its full name, lies on a narrow strip of land between the Dniester river and Ukraine. The territory broke away from Soviet Moldova in the early 1990s amid armed clashes. It is claimed by Moldova and is not recognised by any UN member states.

———— IMPERIAL MEASURES ————

3 barleycorns .... 1 inch
4 inches .... 1 hand
9 inches .... 1 span
12 inches .... 1 foot
3 feet .... 1 yard
2 yards .... 1 fathom

5.5 yards ...... 1 rod, pole or perch
4 rods .... 1 chain
10 chains .... 1 furlong
8 furlongs .... 1 mile
3 miles .... 1 league

NAUTICAL AND GEOGRAPHICAL MEASURES

6 feet .... 1 fathom
110 fathoms .... 1 furlong
6076 feet .... 1 nautical mile (1.15 statute miles)
1 nautical mile .... 1 minute of latitude
60 minutes .... 1 degree of latitude

TROY WEIGHTS
Traditionally used to measure precious metals and gemstones.

24 grains .... 1 pennyweight
20 pennyweights ..... 1 troy ounce

12 troy ounces .... 1 troy pound

DRY MEASURES

4 gills ....1 pint
2 pints .... 1 quart
2 quarts .... 1 pottle
4 quarts .... 1 gallon

2 gallons .... 1 peck
4 pecks .... 1 bushel
3 bushels .... 1 sack

WINE MEASURES

4 gills .... 1 pint
2 pints .... 1 quart
4 quarts .... 1 gallon

18 gallons .... 1 runlet
84 gallons .... 1 puncheon
252 gallons .... 1 tun

BEER MEASURES

2 pints .... 1 quart
4 quarts .... 1 gallon
9 gallons .... 1 firkin
2 firkins .... 1 kilderkin

2 kilderkins .... 1 barrel
1.5 barrels .... 1 hogshead
3 barrels .... 1 butt

PAPER MEASURES

25 sheets (formerly 24 sheets) ... 1 quire	2 reams .... 1 bundle
20 quires .... 1 ream	5 bundles .... 1 bale

---

OF COURSE I'VE READ IT

Mark Twain defined a "classic" as "something that everybody wants to have read and nobody wants to read". These, according to a World Book Day survey, are the books we most lie about having read.

Nineteen Eighty-Four by George Orwell
War and Peace by Leo Tolstoy
Ulysses by James Joyce
The Bible
Madame Bovary by Gustave Flaubert
A Brief History of Time by Stephen Hawking
Midnight's Children by Salman Rushdie
Remembrance of Things Past by Marcel Proust
Dreams from My Father by Barack Obama
The Selfish Gene by Richard Dawkins

CITIES ON THE MUSICAL MAP

Symphonies known by place names.

Leningrad (Symphony No. 7 in C major) by Dmitri Shostakovich
Linz (Symphony No. 36 in C major) by Wolfgang Amadeus Mozart
London (Symphony No. 104 in D major) by Joseph Haydn
London (Symphony No. 2) by Ralph Vaughan Williams
Los Angeles (Symphony No. 4) by Arvo Pärt
New York (Symphony No. 2) by Johan de Meij
Norwich (Symphony No. 2 in A minor) by Edward German
Oxford (Symphony No. 92 in G major) by Haydn
Paris (Symphony No. 31 in D major) by Mozart
Prague (Symphony No. 38 in D major) by Mozart
Rome (Roma Symphony) by Georges Bizet
San Francisco (Symphony No. 8) by Roy Harris

────────────── **FILLING THE EMPTY PLINTH** ──────────────

Since 1999 the plinth at the northwest corner of Trafalgar Square has been used to showcase a series of iconic modern art works.

Mark Wallinger – *Ecce Homo*, 1999. Life-size sculpture of Jesus.

Bill Woodrow – *Regardless of History*, 2000. Giant severed head, topped by a book and a tree.

Rachel Whiteread – *Monument*, 2001. Transparent resin cast of the actual fourth plinth, placed upside down to create a mirror image.

Marc Quinn – *Alison Lapper Pregnant*, 2005–7. 3.5m-high marble sculpture of the artist Alison Lapper, who was born with no arms and shortened legs.

Thomas Schütte – *Model for a Hotel*, 2007. Yellow, red and blue perspex architectural model of a building.

Antony Gormley – *One & Other*, 2009. For 100 days, 24 hours a day, different people stood on the plinth. The 2,400 participants were chosen at random and could use their slot in any way they pleased. One even chose to read a quiz written by this author.

Yinka Shonibare – *Nelson's Ship in a Bottle*, 2010–2. Replica of HMS Victory in an outsized bottle.

Michael Elmgreen and Ingar Dragset – *Powerless Structures, Fig.101*, 2012–13. Gold-coloured sculpture of a boy astride a rocking horse.

Katharina Fritsch – *Hahn/Cock*, 2013–5. Bright blue sculpture of a cockerel, standing nearly 5m high.

Hans Haacke – *Gift Horse*, 2015–6. Skeletal horse in bronze, based on a drawing by George Stubbs. A live ticker of the London Stock Exchange was attached to its leg.

David Shrigley – *Really Good*, 2016–8. Black sculpture of a giant hand, giving an ironic-looking thumbs up.

—————— WHAT A WONDER-FILLED WORLD ——————

The only one of the ancient Seven Wonders of the World still standing is the Great Pyramid of Giza. An updated list was compiled in 2007 by a Swiss foundation that had collated over 100 million global phone and online votes.

Great Wall of China – around 5,500 miles long (though claimed to be longer) construction began in the 7th century BC and continued for 2,000 years.

Chichén Itzá – city in Mexico's Yucatan peninsula, built by the Mayan people from around the 6th century. It is dominated by a step pyramid.

Colosseum – the site of games, gladiatorial combat and even mock naval battles. Built in Rome in the 1st century AD on the orders of Emperor Vespasian.

Petra – ancient city, located in a remote valley in Jordan.

Machu Picchu – Incan settlement in the Peruvian Andes, rediscovered in 1911 by the archaeologist Hiram Bingham (often cited as a possible model for Indiana Jones).

Taj Mahal – mausoleum in Agra, India. Built by the 17th-century Mughal Emperor Shah Jahan in memory of his wife Mumtaz.

Christ the Redeemer – built in 1920 on top of Mount Corcovado in Rio de Janeiro. Standing 30 metres tall, the statue's arms are outspread, as if signalling a wide in cricket.

—————————— GENE GENIES ——————————

In 1953, Watson and Crick revealed the double helix structure of DNA. This is how we compare, genetically speaking, to some other species.

	Genome size (millions of base pairs)	Number of genes
Human	3,000	20,000
Mouse	2,600	25,000
Maize (corn)	2,300	32,000
Chicken	1,000	18,000
Fruit fly	165	15,000

---------------- **DIGGING THE PAST** ----------------

The destruction caused by ISIS at Palmyra in Syria and ancient sites in Iraq is a stark illustration of the threat to the world's archaeological treasures. But it's not all bad news. These are some of the greatest discoveries of the past decade.

Staffordshire hoard, 2009 – the largest hoard of Anglo-Saxon gold and silver ever discovered. It was found in a field near Lichfield and probably dates to the 6th or 7th century.

Crosby Garrett helmet, 2010 – Roman cavalry helmet, with a full-face visor, found by a metal-detectorist in Cumbria. It was sold at auction for over £2 million.

Cashel Man, 2011 – unearthed in County Laois, Ireland, he was the oldest "bog body" ever found. Dating from the early Bronze Age, around 4,000 years ago, archaeologists think he probably met a violent end.

King Richard III, 2012 – the most celebrated overstay in a car park. The remains of Richard III were discovered in Leicester, 527 years after he was killed at the Battle of Bosworth. And Shakespeare hadn't made it up; he did have a crooked spine, after all.

Homo naledi, 2013 – fossil evidence of an extinct species of humanoid, found in a cave in South Africa. The remains were eventually dated to around 300,000–200,000 years ago, although they were initially thought to be much older. Parts of the skeleton resembled a human, but the skull was only a bit larger than a chimpanzee's.

Astrolabe, 2014 – the earliest known mariner's astrolabe was recovered from a shipwreck off the coast of Oman. The vessel is thought to be the Portuguese ship Esmerelda that sank in 1503 while part of Vasco da Gama's armada to India.

Hidden chambers in Tutankhamen's tomb, 2015 – they have yet to be fully surveyed, but it's hoped they may contain the tomb of the pharaoh's step-mother, the legendary Nefertiti.

Mass grave, Athens, 2016 – 80 skeletons were found in an ancient cemetery; dated by archaeologists to the mid-7th century BC, they were shackled together and assumed to be the victims of a mass execution.

USS Indianapolis, 2017 – the sinking of this heavy cruiser by the Japanese in July 1945 was the greatest loss of life from a single vessel that the US Navy had ever suffered. The ship was torpedoed just after it had visited Tinian Island to deliver parts for the atomic bombs that were dropped on Hiroshima and Nagasaki. A harrowing account of the sinking and its aftermath appeared in the film *Jaws*. Despite many attempts to locate the wreck it lay undiscovered until 2017, when it was found by a team led by Microsoft co-founder Paul Allen.

MILLIONS ON THE MOVE

It's not just swallows and salmon but people, too. These are humanity's greatest annual migrations.

Chinese New Year – the largest annual human migration is caused by Chinese workers heading home for the Spring Festival, the celebration of the Lunar New Year. It is the only time of the year that many will see their families. An estimated 3 billion journeys will be made in the busiest 40 days of travel. Sales of adult nappies reportedly peak around this time, as migrant workers take no chances on packed trains.

Thanksgiving – around 50 million Americans make a journey of over 50 miles during Thanksgiving each November.

Arba'een – the world's biggest annual religious pilgrimage. Around 20 million Shia Muslims walk all or part of the 80km between the Iraqi cities of Najaf and Karbala. The gathering marks the end of the 40-day mourning period for the Prophet Muhammad's grandson, Hussein ibn Ali.

Hajj – the Islamic pilgrimage to Mecca in Saudi Arabia is made by over 2 million people each year. It is considered a religious duty for all Muslims who are able to make the journey at least once in their lifetimes.

---------- **RIOT AT THE RITE** ----------

Milestones of modern classical music.

Arnold Schoenberg, *String Quartet No.2* – a landmark in musical modernism, begun in 1907. In the final movement the Austrian-born composer moved away from Western musical traditions and introduced an atonal harmonic structure.

Igor Stravinsky, *The Rite of Spring* – the premiere of Stravinsky's pagan Russia-inspired ballet *The Rite of Spring* took place on 29 May 1913 in Paris. What happened next is often described as a "riot". This is probably an exaggeration but Stravinsky's avant-garde music and Nijinsky's choreography did unsettle much of the audience and a vocal minority was outraged.

Samuel Barber, *Adagio for Strings* – the first performance in 1938 was conducted by Toscanini. An evocative work, it was publicly broadcast in the US after the deaths of Franklin D. Roosevelt and John F. Kennedy. More recently it memorably featured on the soundtracks to the films *The Elephant Man* and *Platoon*.

Dmitri Shostakovich, *Symphony No. 7* – dedicated to the besieged city of Leningrad on its completion in 1941. It came to symbolise resistance to Nazi tyranny and the wartime spirit and sacrifice of the Soviet people.

John Cage, *4'33"* – a piece that literally anyone can play. Premiered in 1952, it consists of musicians sitting in silence.

Benjamin Britten, *War Requiem* – Britten interspersed the Latin Mass with works by the war poet Wilfred Owen. It was first performed in 1962, for the consecration of the new Coventry cathedral. The album recording was an unexpected best-seller.

Karlheinz Stockhausen, *Helikopter-Streichquartett* – an experimental work par excellence. A full performance requires not only a string quartet and audio-visual equipment but four airborne helicopters.

THINKING MORE CLEARLY

The idea of cognitive biases was developed in the 1970s by Israeli psychologists Amos Tversky and Daniel Kahneman. These are 14 things that commonly lead us to make bad decisions.

Anchoring effect – attaching exaggerated importance to the first piece of information you receive.

Authority bias – over-reliance on the opinion of an authority figure.

Bandwagon effect – ideas are more likely to be adopted if others are seen to have already accepted them.

Confirmation bias – when analysing information, giving extra weight to findings that support your existing preconceptions.

Dunning-Kruger effect – unskilled or incompetent people are slow to recognise their own shortcomings.

Egocentric bias – the interpretation of events that puts you in a more positive light e.g. an individual overestimates their contribution to a group effort.

Endowment effect – the tendency to over-value something, simply because you own it.

Frequency illusion – something that has recently been on one's mind suddenly seems to be popping up everywhere.

Halo effect – when a single characteristic of a person or product affects judgements about unrelated factors.

Hindsight bias – the tendency to see past outcomes as inevitable, even though they would have been hard to predict at the time.

Gambler's fallacy – the error of thinking that future probabilities are influenced by past events e.g. the odds of a coin toss are always 50/50, even if heads has come up ten times in a row.

Ostrich effect – simply ignoring negative or unwelcome information.

Projection bias – people tend to overestimate the extent to which others agree with them.

Recency bias – attaching a disproportionate level of importance to the most recent experience.

IT'S COMING FROM OUTER SPACE

We think the dinosaurs were wiped out by an asteroid hitting Earth. In 1908 a comet fragment or meteoroid explosion flattened a 2,000 square km area of Siberian forest around Tunguska. And in 2013 a meteor lit up the skies and shattered windows over Chelyabinsk in Russia. The Torino Scale is an attempt by astronomers to rank the threats from asteroids, comets and other near-Earth objects.

0: No hazard (colour code: white). The likelihood of a collision is zero, or so low as to be effectively zero.

1: Normal (green). Routine discovery predicted to pass near the Earth and pose no unusual level of danger. No cause for public attention or concern. New observations will very likely lead to re-assessing the threat to zero.

2: Meriting attention by astronomers (yellow). Discovery of an object making a somewhat close, but not highly unusual, pass near the Earth. An actual collision is very unlikely.

3: Meriting attention by astronomers (yellow). Close encounter. Current information suggests a 1% or greater chance of collision capable of localised destruction. New telescopic observations will probably reduce the risk level to zero. Attention by the public and officials is merited if the encounter is less than a decade away.

4: Meriting attention by astronomers (yellow). Current calculations give a 1% or greater chance of a collision capable of regional devastation. Again, likely to be re-assessed as a level 0 threat.

5: Threatening (orange). Close encounter posing a serious, but still uncertain, threat of regional devastation. If the impact is less than a decade away, government contingency planning is merited.

6: Threatening (orange). Large object posing a serious, but still uncertain, threat of a global catastrophe. Government planning warranted if the collision is less than 30 years away.

7: Threatening (orange). A very close encounter by a large object. If it is to occur this century, it poses an unprecedented, but still uncertain, threat of a global catastrophe.

8: Certain collisions (red). A collision is certain, capable of causing localised destruction for an impact over land, or possibly a tsunami if close offshore. Such events occur on average between once per 50 years and once per several thousand years.

9: Certain collisions (red). Collision is certain, capable of causing unprecedented regional devastation on land or the threat of a major tsunami if hitting the ocean. Such events occur on average between once per 10,000 years and once per 100,000 years.

10: Certain collisions (red). A collision is certain, capable of causing global climatic catastrophe that may threaten the future of civilisation as we know it. Such events occur on average once per 100,000 years, or more infrequently.

Since the scale was devised in the 1990s the highest ever Torino rating was a 4, given to the asteroid Apophis in 2004. It was subsequently downgraded to a 1. The Tunguska event would have been placed at 8 on the Torino scale.

—————————— **DODGY DEFINITIONS** ——————————

There is a useful rule of thumb in etymology: it's probably not an acronym. These are words that have all been falsely claimed to be acronyms.

Coma	cessation of motor activity
Cop	constable on patrol
Fuck	for unlawful carnal knowledge
Golf	gentlemen only; ladies forbidden
News	north, east, west, south
Nylon	New York, London
Pom	prisoner of Mother England
Posh	port out, starboard home
Shit	ship high in transit

———— STARS OF SOCIAL MEDIA ————

**The most-followed and most-liked people on
Twitter, Instagram and Facebook.**

INSTAGRAM FOLLOWERS (as of August, 2018)

Selena Gomez	140m	Kylie Jenner	113m
Cristiano Ronaldo	139m	Dwayne "The Rock" Johnson	113m
Ariana Grande	125m	Taylor Swift	111m
Beyoncé	117m	Justin Bieber	102m
Kim Kardashian	115m	Neymar	101m

Kylie Jenner's announcement in February 2018 that she'd named her baby Stormi Webster is the most popular picture ever on Instagram with over 17 million likes.

FACEBOOK LIKES (as of August, 2018)

Cristiano Ronaldo	122m	Lionel Messi	90m
Shakira	102m	Eminem	88m
Vin Diesel	99m		

TWITTER FOLLOWERS (as of August, 2018)

Katy Perry	107m	Ellen DeGeneres	76m
Justin Bieber	104m	Lady Gaga	76m
Barack Obama	102m	Cristiano Ronaldo	74m
Rihanna	87m	Justin Timberlake	64m
Taylor Swift	83m	Kim Kardashian	58m

First to 1,000,000 Twitter followers: Ashton Kutcher, 2009
First to 10,000,000 followers: Lady Gaga, 2011
First to 100,000,000 followers: Katy Perry, 2017

The official KFC account only follows 11 people: the five Spice Girls and six men called Herb.

GRAND THEFT ART

Great paintings that have been stolen and are still missing.

Nativity with St Francis and St Lawrence by Caravaggio – stolen in 1969 from a church in Palermo, Sicily.

Francis Bacon by Lucian Freud – in 1988 at the Neue Nationalgalerie in Berlin, Freud's portrait of his friend and fellow artist was snatched in broad daylight. Although Freud designed his own "wanted" poster for the artwork, it has never been recovered.

Storm on the Sea of Galilee by Rembrandt – Rembrandt's only known seascape, taken in 1990 as part of the art heist at Boston's Isabella Stewart Gardner Museum. Also stolen that night was:

The Concert by Johannes Vermeer – one of only 34 paintings that can be unquestionably attributed to the Dutch artist Vermeer. It is considered to be the world's most valuable missing painting. To date, no one has been arrested or charged in connection with the Boston theft and none of the 13 artworks taken has been recovered.

View of Auvers-sur-Oise by Paul Cézanne – stolen from Oxford's Ashmolean Museum on New Year's Eve, 1999. The firework display to mark the new millennium masked the sound of the break-in.

Le pigeon aux petits pois by Pablo Picasso – stolen from the Paris Museum of Modern Art in 2010 along with works by Matisse, Braque and Modigliani. When later apprehended, the thief claimed that he had panicked and placed the painting in a rubbish bin. It has never been found.

Portrait of a Lady by Gustav Klimt – last seen at the Ricci Oddi Gallery of Modern Art in Piacenza, Italy, in 1997.

Poppy Flowers (Vase and Flowers) by Vincent Van Gogh – stolen for the first time in 1977 from Cairo's Mahmoud Khalil Museum and recovered in Kuwait a decade later. It was stolen again from the same Cairo gallery in 2010 and is still missing.

MEDICAL MYTHS

Fake health news and old wives' tales.

Cold weather causes colds – true, they're called "colds" but they're caused by viruses rather than changes in temperature.

Vaccines cause autism – a pernicious myth, originating in a study published in 1998 by the now-discredited doctor Andrew Wakefield.

We only use 10% of our brains – the myth of unfulfilled potential is comforting, but it's not supported by the evidence of brain scans.

Stress causes ulcers – they are chiefly caused by helicobacter pylori bacteria.

Sugar makes children hyperactive – studies suggest that it's the situation (e.g. birthday parties, break times, etc) that causes children to get over-excited rather than the sugar itself.

You should drink 2.5 litres of water a day – we need the water, but most of it is contained in the food we eat.

Don't swim just after you've eaten – cramps can come at any time and are not linked to eating and digestion.

Most of your body heat is lost through the head – only because it is often left exposed to the elements. The head is no more susceptible to losing heat than any other part of the body.

You're eating for two in pregnancy – an expectant mother needs to eat a little more, but will only need an extra 200 calories a day in the last three months of the pregnancy.

Hair and nails continue growing after death – they don't, but the skin around the nails or on the scalp may retract slightly giving the impression of continued growth.

Knuckle cracking causes arthritis – the sound is caused by the release of air bubbles in the joints and no medical research has proven a link to osteoarthritis.

Chewing gum stays in the stomach for 7 years – the body can't break down gum as it does other food, but it does pass through the digestive system and is excreted.

———— DUE TO UNFORESEEN CIRCUMSTANCES... ————

The record books are packed full of things that actually happened. Here are some events that didn't.

1916 Berlin Olympics – cancelled because of the First World War.

Edward VIII's coronation – scheduled for 12 May 1937, the mugs, coins and other memorabilia had already been manufactured when he abdicated the throne in December 1936. The date was kept for the coronation of his brother George VI.

1940 Tokyo Olympics and 1944 London Olympics – the outbreak of the Second World War caused these games to be abandoned. The Winter Olympics scheduled for 1940 in Sapporo, Japan and 1944 in Cortina d'Ampezzo, Italy also never happened.

1955 Trooping the Colour – the traditional celebration of military pomp and pageantry to mark the Queen's official birthday was cancelled because of a national train strike.

1975 World Chess Championship – the Cold War match-up between American Bobby Fischer and the Russian Anatoly Karpov never happened after a dispute over the format of the competition.

1986 World Cup in Colombia – FIFA had originally awarded the tournament to Colombia but the South American nation pulled out as hosts in 1982 because of an economic crisis.

1994 World Series – baseball's showpiece event was cancelled for only the second time (firstly in 1904) because of an ongoing strike by the players' association.

2001 Cheltenham Festival – an outbreak of foot-and-mouth in Britain forced the abandonment of the horse racing festival.

2004–05 NHL season – no professional ice hockey was played and the Stanley Cup was not awarded. A dispute between players and owners over a salary cap led to the cancellation of an entire season of a major North American sports league for the first time.

2010 Islamic Solidarity Games – cancelled after a dispute between hosts Iran and its Arab neighbours over whether to call the Gulf waterway "Persian" or "Arabian".

——— STORMY WEATHER ———

From sea as flat as a mill pond to storms on the scale of Hurricane
Katrina, all scenarios are covered in these weather scales.

BEAUFORT WIND FORCE SCALE

0 .... Calm (wind speed <1mph)
1 .... Light air (1–3mph)
2 .... Light breeze (4–7mph)
3 .... Gentle breeze (8–12mph)
4 ... Moderate breeze (13–18mph)
5 .... Fresh breeze (19–24mph)
6 .... Strong breeze (25–31mph)

7 .... Near gale (32–38mph)
8 .... Gale (39–46mph)
9 .... Strong gale (47–54mph)
10 .... Storm (55–63mph)
11 ...... Violent storm (64–72mph)
12 .... Hurricane (73+mph)

SAFFIR–SIMPSON HURRICANE WIND SCALE

1 ...... Very dangerous winds will
produce some damage
(74–95mph)
2 .... Extremely dangerous winds
will cause extensive damage
(96–110mph)

3 ... (major) Devastating damage
will occur (111–129mph)
4 .. (major) Catastrophic damage
will occur (130–156mph)
5 .. (major) Catastrophic damage
will occur (157+mph)

ENHANCED FUJITA SCALE (TORNADO INTENSITY)

0 ..... Minor damage (65–85mph)
1 ... Moderate damage (86–110mph)
2 .... Considerable damage
(111–135mph)

3 .. Severe damage (136–165mph)
4 .... Devastating damage
(166–200mph)
5 .. Incredible damage (200+mph)

DOUGLAS SEA SCALE

0 .... Calm (glassy) (no waves)
1........................... Calm (rippled)
(wave height 0–0.1m)
2 .. Smooth (wavelets) (0.1–0.5m)
3 .... Slight (0.5–1.25m)
4 .... Moderate (1.25–2.5m)

5 .... Rough (2.5–4m)
6 .... Very rough (4–6m)
7 .... High (6–9m)
8 .... Very high (9–14m)
9 .... Phenomenal (14+m)

PET PIN-UPS

The influencers of the animal world.

Grumpy Cat – the cat that launched a thousand memes. If, as they say, the Internet is for cats, then Tardar Sauce is its queen. Her permanently cross expression, caused by an underbite and dwarfism, helped make her an online sensation. She even starred in her own Christmas film in 2014.

Dolly the Sheep – a scientific pioneer. She was born in 1996, the first mammal to be successfully cloned from an adult cell. Named after Dolly Parton (she was cloned from a mammary cell) her preserved body is now on display at the National Museum of Scotland in Edinburgh.

Cecil the Lion – the trophy-killing of Cecil, an African lion, by a US dentist and recreational hunter sparked international outrage in 2015.

Meredith Grey and Olivia Benson – the cats that belong to the singer Taylor Swift. They are named after the lead female characters in the TV series *Grey's Anatomy* and *Law & Order: Special Victims Unit*.

Choupette – Karl Lagerfeld's pampered puss. She has over 100,000 followers on Instagram and earns millions each year in modelling fees.

Naruto – the Indonesian macaque who took a celebrated selfie with a camera belonging to wildlife photographer David Slater. A legal battle ensued over who owned the copyright to the photo: the monkey or the man? Judges eventually decided it was the latter.

Asia, Koji and Gustavo – Lady Gaga's pet bulldogs, who have appeared on the cover of *Harper's Bazaar* magazine and notched up a quarter of a million Instagram followers.

Jiff – the fastest dog on two legs. A talented (and uncommonly cute) Pomeranian dog, who won Guinness World Records for walking on his hind legs and front paws. He's also the world's most popular animal on social media with 25 million followers.

———————— THE FINE ART OF BEING WRONG ————————

Terrible predictions, bad advice and dodgy dossiers.

Dewey Defeats Truman
Headline in the *Chicago Daily Tribune* newspaper, proclaiming
victory for Thomas E. Dewey over Harry S. Truman in the 1948 US
presidential election. Truman had, in fact, won a comfortable victory.

"Television won't last. It's a flash in the pan."
Mary Somerville, BBC head of education, in 1948.

"Guitar groups are on the way out."
Decca records, turning down The Beatles after their audition on
1 January 1962.

**"We are not about to send American boys nine or ten thousand
miles away from home to do what Asian boys ought to be doing
for themselves."**
Lyndon B. Johnson, two weeks before winning the 1964 US
presidential election. More than 58,000 American servicemen would
die in Vietnam in the war that Johnson subsequently escalated.

Iraq's Weapons of Mass Destruction
Controversial 2002 British government report on Saddam Hussein's
chemical, biological and nuclear weapons programmes. Largely
based on bogus intelligence, the claims in the "dodgy dossier"
have subsequently proved to be false.

"There are no American infidels in Baghdad. Never!"
Muhammad al-Sahhaf, Minister of Information, during the 2003
invasion of Iraq. His relentlessly upbeat, verging on the delusional,
assessment of the state of Saddam Hussein's prospects earned him
the nickname "Comical Ali".

"Spam will be a thing of the past in two years' time."
Microsoft founder Bill Gates, speaking at the Davos World Economic
Forum in 2004. Fourteen years later, well over half of
all email traffic worldwide is spam.

"Next Christmas, the iPod will be dead, finished, gone, kaput."
Alan Sugar, founder of Amstrad, in a 2005 interview. Nearly 40 million iPods were sold in 2006, with sales peaking at 54 million units in 2008.

"There's no chance that the iPhone is going to get any significant market share. No chance."
Steve Ballmer, Microsoft CEO, in 2007. Another Apple sceptic proved spectacularly wrong. Within five years, iPhone sales alone had overtaken Microsoft's overall revenue.

EUREKA!

Historic moments that happened at bath time.

Archimedes' inspiration – the original "eureka" moment. The ancient Greek mathematician supposedly formulated his eponymous principle while getting into the bath. He noticed that a body immersed in a fluid is pushed up by a force equal to the weight of the displaced fluid. According to legend he ran naked into the street to share the news of his discovery.

Jean-Paul Marat's assassination – the French revolutionary took regular medicinal baths to alleviate a skin condition. On 13 July 1793 he was visited by Charlotte Corday, a supporter of a rival faction, and stabbed to death while he bathed. In death, he became a revolutionary martyr and he was depicted as a Christ-like figure in Jacques-Louis David's propaganda painting *The Death of Marat*.

Deaths of singers – Jim Morrison, lead singer of The Doors, was found dead in the bathtub of his Paris flat in 1971. The troubled diva Whitney Houston accidentally drowned in her bath at the Beverly Hilton Hotel on 11 February 2012.

Presidential soak – US President Howard Taft certainly loved a bath, but never got stuck in the tub, as claimed in a popular myth. For a 1908 voyage to the Panama Canal, a bath was specially commissioned for Taft to use on board ship. It was seven feet long and weighed a ton. Equally capacious baths were installed in the White House when he assumed the presidency.

THE JAWBONE OF AN ASS

Gruesome and outlandish deaths in the Bible.

Abel – the first murder victim, killed by his brother Cain (Genesis 4).

Korah – swallowed up by the earth for leading a revolt against Moses. Fire then consumed 250 of his followers (Numbers 16).

Sisera – Canaanite commander who was offered food and refuge by a woman called Jael. When he was asleep she hammered a tent peg through his temple (Judges 5).

Abimelech – his head was crushed by a millstone dropped by a woman from the walls of a city he was besieging. Realising the wound was mortal he ordered his armour-bearer to finish him off, so that it couldn't be said that he had been killed by a woman (Judges 9).

1,000 Philistines – slain by Samson using only the jawbone of an ass (Judges 15).

Eli – fell off his chair and died when he heard that the Ark of the Covenant had been captured by the Philistines (1 Samuel 4).

Absalom – his luxuriant hair got entangled in an oak tree and he was stabbed to death (2 Samuel 18).

42 jeering children of Bethel – torn apart by two bears for mocking the prophet Elisha's baldness (2 Kings 2).

Jezebel – died after being thrown out of a window by her own eunuchs. Her body was then eaten by stray dogs, as predicted by the prophet Elijah (2 Kings 9).

Haman – hanged on the very gallows that he had erected to execute Mordecai (Esther 8).

John the Baptist – executed reluctantly by King Herod to honour an oath to the daughter of Herodias. His head was served up on a platter at the king's birthday feast (Matthew 14).

Eutychus – nodded off while listening to a long sermon by St Paul and fell to his death from an open window. But there was a happy ending; he was resurrected in time for dinner (Acts 20).

———— GET OFF OF MY CLOUD ————

The classification of clouds into types was first proposed by the amateur meteorologist Luke Howard in 1802. In 2017, for the first time in 30 years, 12 new cloud types were added to the International Cloud Atlas.

Asperitas – rarely seen, wave-like clouds.

Volutus – also called a roll cloud: long, low and horizontal.

Homogenitus – clouds created by human activity, such as aircraft vapour trails.

Cavum – circular hole in a thin layer of supercooled water droplet cloud.

Flumen – bands of low clouds associated with a severe convective storm.

Murus – a wall cloud, associated with severe storms.

Cauda – horizontal, tail-shaped cloud, typically attached to a wall cloud.

Cataractagenitus – clouds developing around large waterfalls.

Silvagenitus – clouds appearing over forests.

Flammagenitus – clouds caused by volcanic activity, wildfire or forest fires.

Fluctus – clouds resembling curls or breaking waves.

Homomutatus – formed when persistent vapour trails are spread out over the sky by strong winds.

———— GOING ROUND IN CIRCLES 2 ————

The countries you pass through while travelling along some of the Earth's imaginary lines.

Tropic of Cancer (East from the prime meridian)

Algeria • Niger • Libya • Egypt • Saudi Arabia • UAE • Oman • India • Bangladesh • Myanmar • China • Taiwan • Mexico • Bahamas • Western Sahara/Morocco • Mauritania • Mali

—— THE GERMANS ALMOST CERTAINLY HAVE A WORD FOR IT ——

Untranslatable words, often connected with melancholy.

Desenrascanço – Portuguese, loosely means "disentanglement" but is used for the art of finding an elegant, ingenious solution to a difficult problem.

Entrecejo – Spanish, for the space between the eyebrows.

L'ésprit d'escalier – French, for the feeling when you've thought of the perfect riposte, long after the chance to make it has passed. Literally meaning "staircase wit", it was coined in the 18th century by the philosopher Denis Diderot.

Flâneur – French, for a man who saunters about town, observing society.

Gattara – Italian, for an old lady who is devoted to feeding stray cats.

Gemütlich – German, meaning pleasant, genial and good-natured.

Irusu – Japanese, pretending to be out when someone calls.

Kuidaore – Japanese, meaning to become broke because you've spent all your money on food and drink.

Poshlost – Russian, meaning vulgarity, tackiness or banality.

Saudade – Portuguese, a feeling of longing, melancholy or nostalgia.

Schadenfreude – German word (literally "sorrow joy") for the malicious enjoyment of other people's misfortunes.

Sehnsucht – German for a wistful longing.

Shinrin-yoku – Japanese, literally a "forest bath", meaning the restorative effects of a walk in the woods.

Sobremesa – Spanish, for the time spent sitting round the table and conversing after a meal.

Toska – Russian word, suggesting emotional pain or pangs of melancholy. In his translation of Pushkin's *Eugene Onegin*, Vladimir Nabokov wrote "No single word in English renders all the shades of toska".

Tsundoku – Japanese word that combines the characters for "pile up" and "read". It means the acquisition of books that will probably never be read.

Weltschmerz – German, referring to a weary or pessimistic feeling about life. Literally means "world pain".

──────── IS THAT YOUR FINAL ANSWER? ────────

Five people have won the top prize on the UK quiz show *Who Wants to be a Millionaire?* These are their final questions to win the jackpot (correct answers on page 141).

1. Which King was married to Eleanor of Aquitaine?
   a) Henry I b) Henry II c) Richard I d) Henry V

2. If you planted the seeds of Quercus robur, what would grow?
   a) Trees b) Flowers c) Vegetables d) Grain

3. Which scientific unit is named after an Italian nobleman?
   a) Pascal b) Ohm c) Volt d) Hertz

4. Which of these is not one of the American Triple Crown horse races?
   a) Arlington Million b) Belmont Stakes
   c) Kentucky Derby d) Preakness Stakes

5. Which boxer was famous for striking the gong in the introduction to J. Arthur Rank films?
   a) Bombardier Billy Wells b) Freddie Mills c) Terry Spinks d) Don Cockell

──────── THE MEASURE OF MEASUREMENTS ────────

How SI base units are defined by the International Bureau of Weights and Measures.

Metre – Length of the path travelled by light in vacuum during a time interval of 1/299,792,458 of a second.

Second – The duration of 9,192,631,770 periods of the radiation corresponding to the transition between the two hyperfine levels of the ground state of the caesium 133 atom.

Kilogram – Unit of mass, equal to the mass of the international prototype of the kilogram (a cylinder of platinum-iridium alloy kept by the Bureau at its HQ in France).

——————— THE ORIGIN OF SUPER SPECIES ———————

Dosed by radiation, transformed by pure willpower or just born that way, here's how some iconic superheroes got their powers.

Spider-Man – Peter Parker acquired his superpowers and spidey sense after being bitten by a radioactive spider. The murder of his uncle Ben by a burglar motivated him to fight crime.

The Hulk – Dr Bruce Banner absorbed a huge dose of gamma rays during the detonation of an experimental bomb. The result was strength (and a temper) that could only be described as incredible.

Fantastic Four – four astronauts were exposed to cosmic rays during a test flight in Reed Richards' experimental rocket ship. The massive doses of radiation mutated the quartet in varying ways.

Superman – born Kal-El on the planet Krypton, he was sent here when his home world was threatened with destruction. On Earth, he has powers that include flight, extraordinary strength, X-ray vision and super hearing. As long as he stays away from kryptonite.

Black Panther – T'Challa was born into the royal family of the African country of Wakanda. After his father was killed by the evil Klaw, T'Challa claimed the throne and defeated the incumbent to become the Black Panther. Taking the mysterious heart-shaped herb boosted his speed, strength and agility to superhuman levels.

X-Men – a group of genetically mutated humans, born with superpowers. They were first encountered as teenagers at Xavier's School for Gifted Youngsters.

Captain America – during World War Two, Steve Rogers was rejected by the army for his small size but agreed to test a serum that transformed him into a super-charged warrior.

Wonder Woman – or Princess Diana of Themyscira, Daughter of Hippolyta, to give her full title. Her abilities were a mixture of god-given (literally) powers and rigorous Amazonian training.

Iron Man – during the Vietnam War, the playboy industrialist Tony Stark was captured by a Viet Cong warlord and ordered to build weapons to aid the Communist effort. Instead, he built his powered metal suit and made his escape.

Batman – as a child, Bruce Wayne witnessed his parents' murder by a mugger. At their graveside, he swore vengeance on criminals. Using his vast family fortune and a fearsome training regimen he transformed himself into the vigilante superhero Batman.

Daredevil – saving a man from an oncoming truck, Matt Murdock was exposed to radioactive materials. He was left blinded, but his other senses were enhanced and he developed a form of radar vision.

FAST FOOD NATIONS

In 2010, sandwich maker Subway overtook McDonald's to become the world's biggest restaurant chain. These are the top international fast food outlets, by number of establishments.

Business	Number of outlets	Countries/territories
Subway	44,600	112
McDonald's	36,900	118
Starbucks	27,300	75
KFC	20,500	125
Pizza Hut	16,800	120
Burger King	16,000	100+
Domino's Pizza	13,800	85

McDonald's serves around 68 million people each day, a little under 1% of the world's entire population. The Big Mac (originally called the Aristocrat) was first introduced in Pittsburgh in 1967. Now, 900 million are sold a year worldwide.

The sandwiches Subway makes each year, laid end-to-end, would stretch around the globe 14 times. Pizza Hut can claim to have gone one better, taking its business literally out of this world. In 2001, it delivered a pizza to the cosmonaut Yuri Usachov on the International Space Station.

--------------- **JUMPING ON THE BANNED WAGON** ---------------

The Catholic Church's notorious list of forbidden books, the Index Librorum Prohibitorum, was abandoned in 1966. But books continue to be banned by governments and religious authorities. These are some more recent works that have fallen foul of the censors.

The Satanic Verses by Salman Rushdie. Alleged insults to the Prophet Muhammad earned the author death threats and a fatwa from the Iranian spiritual leader Ayatollah Khomeini. Rushdie spent the next few years in hiding under the name Joseph Anton. The book was banned across the Islamic world.

Lord Horror by David Britton. In 1989, this lurid novel about the Nazi propagandist William Joyce became the last book to be seized and banned under the UK's Obscene Publications Act.

American Psycho by Bret Easton Ellis. Published in 1991, this savage satire of consumerism was banned in the Australian state of Queensland for its violent content.

Wild Swans by Jung Chang. A family history of modern China, told through three generations of women. The book was a worldwide bestseller but remains banned in China itself, although it is available in Hong Kong.

The Da Vinci Code by Dan Brown. Banned in Lebanon in 2004 after complaints it was offensive to Christians. It was also banned in the small Indian state of Nagaland. The offence was caused by the suggestion that Jesus fathered a child with Mary Magdalene.

Fifty Shades of Grey by E.L. James. The bestselling erotic novel and its sequels *Fifty Shades Darker* and *Fifty Shades Freed* were banned in Malaysia on the grounds that they were a "threat to morality". *Fifty Shades* was also considered too racy for the residents of Brevard County, Florida and was removed from the local library's shelves.

Thirteen Reasons Why by Jay Asher. The American Library Association publishes an annual list of the most frequently challenged and banned books in US schools and libraries. In 2017, the top spot belonged to this young adult novel because of its theme of a high school student's suicide.

─────── UNEASY LIES THE HEAD THAT WEARS A CROWN ───────

A coronation last took place in the UK on 2 June 1953, so here's a reminder how a British monarch is crowned.

The Procession – from Buckingham Palace to Westminster Abbey, where coronations have taken place for over 900 years. The service is based on the one used for the coronation of King Edgar at Bath in 973.

The Recognition and the Oath – the people, as represented by the congregation, acclaim their sovereign. The new monarch swears an oath, administered by the Archbishop of Canterbury, to uphold the law and protect the Church of England.

The Anointing – the archbishop pours aromatic holy oil from the ampulla into the coronation spoon and anoints the monarch on the palms, breast and head. Dating to the 12th century, the coronation spoon is the oldest object in the Crown Jewels. The medieval coronation regalia was broken up or melted down by the Commonwealth government after the execution of Charles I in 1649.

The Investiture and Crowning – the monarch is dressed in the coronation robes and presented with golden spurs, a symbol of chivalry. A jewelled sword and the orb are offered to the monarch and then placed on the altar. The coronation ring is put on the fourth finger of their right hand and sceptres are held in each hand. St Edward's crown is placed on the sovereign's head by the archbishop.

The Enthroning and Homage – the monarch rises from St Edward's chair and sits on a raised throne. Here, they receive homage from the clergy and the nobles. The coronation crown is exchanged for the Imperial state crown and the newly crowned monarch processes from the abbey.

Queen Elizabeth II's coronation was the first to be televised and was watched by 27 million people in the UK. A further 3 million lined the streets of London.

——————— ARCHITECTURE FOR ART'S SAKE ———————

The designs of high-profile "starchitects", these galleries and museums are works of art themselves.

Guggenheim Museum, New York – it opened in 1959, six months after the death of its creator, the architect Frank Lloyd Wright. The concrete spiral design made it an iconic work of modern architecture.

Centre Georges Pompidou, Paris – the newspaper *Le Figaro* was not exactly keen on the building: "Paris has its own monster, just like Loch Ness." But 40 years since it opened in 1977, the Pompidou Centre, designed by the then unknown architects Richard Rogers and Renzo Piano, is now a cherished landmark. A provincial branch was established in Metz in 2010.

Tate Modern, London – it was not a new building, in fact, but the old Bankside power station on the south side of the Thames. Designed by Giles Gilbert Scott, who was also responsible for Battersea power station, it ceased operations in 1981 and the building was threatened with demolition. After a conversion led by the architects Herzog & de Meuron, it opened to the public in 2000. In its first year it attracted 5 million visitors, making it the most popular modern art museum in the world.

Guggenheim Museum, Bilbao – Frank Gehry's design was described by the doyen of modern architecture Philip Johnson as the "greatest building of our time". A series of interconnected galleries, sheathed in titanium, it was built in the run-down port area of Bilbao and opened in 1997. The museum's role in promoting regeneration of the city was labelled the "Bilbao effect". It set a trend for cultural institutions to open architecturally striking outposts in hitherto unglamorous locations.

Ordos Museum, China – a landmark museum for the half-empty "ghost" city of Kangbashi in Inner Mongolia, on the edge of the Gobi Desert.

Louvre Abu Dhabi – designed by Jean Nouvel and opened in 2017 on the Saadiyat Island cultural zone. Abu Dhabi paid over half a billion dollars for the Louvre branding rights. The most expensive painting ever sold, Leonardo da Vinci's *Salvator Mundi*, bought for $450m in 2017, will be displayed in the museum.

NOT SINGLE SPIES, BUT BATTALIONS

It's said that spying is the world's second oldest profession. Anyone who thought that espionage would cease with the end of the Cold War has been proved very wrong.

Noshir Gowadia – he was one of the designers of the propulsion system of the B-2 stealth bomber at the aviation company Northrop. In 2011 he was convicted of selling military secrets to China and sentenced to 32 years in prison. His information had helped the Chinese develop stealth cruise missiles.

Jonathan Pollard – he is the only American to receive a life sentence for spying on behalf of a friendly country. A civilian intelligence analyst, he was arrested in 1985 for passing classified information to Israel, a key US ally. He was paroled in 2015 after serving 28 years of his sentence.

Robert Hanssen – a Department of Justice review in 2002 stated that Hanssen's treason was "possibly the worst intelligence disaster in US history". He was an FBI agent who spied for the Soviet Union and later Russia from 1979 until his arrest in 2001. His work in counter-intelligence gave him access to lists of American agents which he sold to his Soviet handlers. His espionage career coincided with that of another equally damaging spy, Aldrich Ames, a CIA officer who was caught in 1994. Hanssen, like Ames, was sentenced to spend the rest of his life in prison.

Walter Myers – US State Department official who was convicted in 2010 of spying for Cuba for almost 30 years.

Anna Chapman and the Illegals Program – Chapman was part of a loose-knit group of Russian sleeper agents in the US. Posing as normal citizens, their aim was to infiltrate American society and build contacts in business, politics and academia. The group was exposed in 2010 and, in an echo of the Cold War, they were exchanged in Vienna for Russians who had spied for America.

Sergei Skripal – the Russian former British spy and his daughter Yulia were poisoned with a nerve agent at their Salisbury home in 2018. They both survived, but the attempted assassination was blamed on the Russian security services.

--------------- **LEFT ON THE DRAWING BOARD** ---------------

Folies de grandeur or visionary statements ahead of their time, these buildings never made it past the planning stage.

Palace of the Soviets – in the early 1930s, Boris Iofan won the contest to design Moscow's Palace of the Soviets, an administrative and congress centre to be built on the site of the demolished Cathedral of Christ the Saviour. His neoclassical design resembled a giant wedding cake, over 400m high, topped by an enormous statue of Lenin. The outbreak of war halted construction on the Palace of the Soviets and the foundations were later converted into the world's largest open-air swimming pool.

Germania – mercifully, the Third Reich only lasted 12 years, rather than the millennium envisaged by Hitler. If it had survived longer, the Führer would have realised his plans to refashion Berlin as a new Nazi capital called Germania. Hitler's favourite architect Albert Speer produced plans for a monumental new city, comprising wide boulevards, triumphal arches and huge public squares. The most ambitious building was the *Volkshalle* (People's Hall), based on the Pantheon in Rome. At nearly 300m high, its dome was to have a diameter of 250m. That's big enough to have its own microclimate and for the entire dome of St Peter's in the Vatican to fit through the oculus, the circular opening at the top.

Phare du Monde – the "lighthouse of the world" was planned for the 1937 World Fair in Paris. It was to be a 700m tall tower that could be driven up by cars along a spiral track on the outside. The top of the tower had a restaurant and ample parking, of course.

The Illinois – in 1957, two years before his death, architect Frank Lloyd Wright outlined a project for a mile-high 528-storey skyscraper. It would be built in Chicago and would be four times higher than the Empire State Building. Although it never came to fruition, the design has a tangible legacy. The current world's tallest building, the Burj Khalifa in Dubai, is said to have been inspired by the plans for The Illinois.

Shimizu Mega-City Pyramid and X-Seed 4000 – a 2,000m high pyramid and a tower reaching 4km, both of these projects were envisaged for the greater Tokyo area. They would provide living space for hundreds of thousands of people and would be the largest man-made buildings ever constructed. However, the chances of either making it off the drawing board are negligible.

───── MEMORABLE MNEMONICS ─────

We all know why Richard of York gave battle in vain but here are some other aids to the memory.

All beheadings should carry heavy penalties – six wives of Henry VIII (Aragon, Boleyn, Seymour, Cleves, Howard, Parr).

My very excellent mother just served us nachos – planets of the Solar System (Mercury, Venus, Earth, Mars, Jupiter, Saturn, Uranus, Neptune).

How to punish bad Daleks before many million earthlings truly see clearly why – 12 actors and one actress who have played the Doctor in Doctor Who (Hartnell, Troughton, Pertwee, T. Baker, Davison, C. Baker, McCoy, McGann, Eccleston, Tennant, Smith, Capaldi, Whittaker).

I value xylophones like cows dig milk – Roman numerals in ascending value.

Pegs Law – the Seven Deadly Sins (pride, envy, gluttony, sloth, lust, avarice, wrath).

Do kings play chess on fine green silk – taxonomic classifications in biology (domain, kingdom, phylum, class, order, family, genus, species).

Mrs Gren – processes of living organisms (movement, respiration, sensitivity, growth, reproduction, excretion, nutrition).

Memorisation's never easy; memory often needs initial cues – if you can't remember how to spell mnemonic.

―――――――― **#ACTIVISM IN THE DIGITAL AGE** ――――――――

Protest has moved from the streets onto the Internet.

Anonymous – "hacktivist" group, formed around 2004, that has launched denial-of-service attacks on governments, companies and religious organisations. A loose association of hackers, its targets have included the Westboro Baptist Church, the Church of Scientology, Islamic State, the FBI, the US Justice Department, Mastercard and PayPal.

WikiLeaks – set up by Australian convicted hacker Julian Assange in 2006 to publish secret political information. It has released large caches of documents relating to the wars in Iraq and Afghanistan, and published online over 250,000 diplomatic cables from the US State Department in 2010.

Occupy movement – began in 2011 as Occupy Wall Street, a protest in New York against social and economic injustice. People took over Zuccotti Park in Lower Manhattan, rallying behind the slogan "we are the 99%". The movement rapidly spread and a London camp was established outside St Paul's Cathedral.

Edward Snowden – whistle-blower, who leaked details of secret intelligence-gathering operations by the US and its allies in 2013. An IT contractor for the National Security Agency, Snowden confirmed that US agencies had accessed the data of companies including Facebook, Google and Apple. Snowden was charged with espionage by the US authorities and fled to Moscow.

Black Lives Matter – the movement started on Twitter in 2013 with the hashtag #BlackLivesMatter, created by Alicia Garza, Patrisse Cullors and Opal Tometi. It was inspired by the controversial acquittal of the man who had killed Florida teenager Trayvon Martin. Street protests erupted the following year in Ferguson, Missouri, after the fatal shooting of Michael Brown by a police officer.

Farah Baker – in 2014, 16-year-old Palestinian girl Farah Baker live-tweeted the Israeli bombardment of Gaza. Within days her Twitter following leapt from 800 to 166,000 as she became the human face of the conflict.

#OscarSoWhite – hashtag first used by blogger April Reign in 2015 to draw attention to the under-representation of people of colour in the recent Academy Award nominations.

Everyday Sexism Project, #metoo and Time's Up – campaigns promoting women's rights and opposing sexism and sexual harassment in the workplace and elsewhere. Allegations against film producer Harvey Weinstein gave the movement impetus and a high profile, but its scope was never limited to just Hollywood.

——— RECOMMENDATIONS FOR YOU: HOW NETFLIX WORKS ———

In spring 2018, Netflix passed 125 million subscribers worldwide. This followed the announcement of $8 billion worth of spending on 700 pieces of original content. How are people expected to navigate this maze of film and television? The recommendation system has a big say; more than 80% of the content watched on Netflix is discovered by viewers in this way. This is how it "knows" what people want to watch.

All shows on Netflix are watched first by paid reviewers and manually tagged with any conceivable defining feature e.g. quirky humour, cerebral, subtitles or strong female lead. There are over 1,000 different tags for these professional bingers to choose from. This information is allied with the behaviour of the individual Netflix subscriber: what are they watching, for how long and when? A profile is built up of viewing habits and preferences and the data is crunched by the algorithms. Netflix has identified around 2,000 different viewer taste groups. Everyone will fit into a number of these overlapping categories. This will determine what genre suggestions come up at the top of your screen and exactly how they are presented. If you've got a weakness for, say, Brad Pitt, then his picture will appear in the thumbnails. And as often as not, you keep watching. As a former Netflix data scientist explained "the algorithms know you better than you know yourself".

NOT FOR THE MANTLEPIECE

Awards that nobody wants to win.

Golden Raspberry Awards – the Razzies, as they're popularly known, celebrate the very worst that Hollywood has to offer. Few winners collect their awards in person. Notable exceptions include Sandra Bullock, who won an Oscar for *The Blind Side* the next night and Halle Berry, who accepted the Razzie for *Catwoman* while clutching the Best Actress Academy Award she received for *Monster's Ball*. Erotic drama *Showgirls* and sci-fi dud *Battlefield Earth* won a record seven Razzies each.

Ig Nobel Prizes – organised by the journal *Improbable Research*, the Igs reward scientific work that is seemingly absurd, yet thought-provoking. Past winners include the medical research paper "Why Do Old Men Have Big Ears?", a study into the optimal way to dunk a biscuit in tea and the book *That Gunk on Your Car*, a guide to splattered insect remains on motor vehicles.

Darwin Awards – not to be confused with the Royal Society's prestigious Darwin Medal for biology, these awards "salute the improvement of the human genome by honouring those who accidentally remove themselves from it". Notable recipients are the men (and it's almost always men) who played Russian roulette with a semi-automatic pistol, bungee jumped with a homemade rope, drunkenly stole a plane without knowing how to fly and opened their own letter bomb when it came back "return to sender".

Carbuncle Cup – architecture's wooden spoon, given each year to Britain's worst building. Awarded by *Building Design* magazine, its name was inspired by Prince Charles' comment in 1984 that a proposed extension to the National Gallery looked like a "monstrous carbuncle". Winners include London's "Walkie-Talkie" skyscraper, the Cutty Sark renovation, Liverpool Ferry Terminal and the MediaCity UK complex in Salford.

Bad Sex in Fiction Award – devised by the *Literary Review* magazine, this prize for an outstandingly bad sex scene in a novel has been won by renowned writers such as Norman Mailer, Sebastian Faulks and Tom Wolfe. And Morrissey.

Foot in Mouth and Golden Bull Awards – awarded by the Plain English Campaign for, respectively, the most baffling quotes by public figures and the worst examples of written gobbledygook in official communications.

Lanterne Rouge – the rider who finishes last in the Tour de France.

Mr Irrelevant – the title given to the American football player picked last in the annual NFL draft.

———— FACE WITH TEARS OF JOY: AN EMOJI-NAL STORY ————

More than 60 million emojis are used on Facebook every day. On Messenger, that number swells to 5 billion.

The story of emojis began in Japan in 1999. Shigetaka Kurita had noticed how popular the heart symbol was among pager users and decided to incorporate a visual element into the mobile internet platform he was working on. He drew inspiration from the symbols used in weather forecasts and the Chinese characters in written Japanese. The name "emoji" came from the Japanese words "e" (picture) and "moji" (letter, character).

Initially they were merely seen as a way for teenagers and others with short attention spans to communicate. But emojis have come of age. Oxford Dictionaries raised eyebrows in 2015 by declaring the Face with Tears of Joy emoji as its "word" of the year. It had been the most popular emoji globally and represented 20% of all emojis used in the UK. In her presidential election campaign Hillary Clinton used them to get voter feedback, asking for feelings about student debt "in 3 emojis or less". And in 2016 New York's Museum of Modern Art acquired the original set of 176 emojis produced by the Nippon Telegraph and Telephone company.

As of June 2018, there are 2,823 emojis in the Unicode Standard, with more created every year. The emoji is here to stay.

─────── GAME OF CLONES ───────

Big-budget, bloody and more pirated than any other series, *Game of Thrones* is a TV phenomenon. But what real-life events might have inspired the history buff George R.R. Martin? Here are some suggestions.

Warning: contains spoilers.

Westeros – the seven kingdoms of Westeros echo the so-called Heptarchy of Anglo-Saxon England (East Anglia, Essex, Kent, Mercia, Northumbria, Sussex and Wessex). The vicious contest for the Iron Throne recalls the 15th-century Wars of the Roses; the names of the rival houses of Stark and Lannister mirror those of York and Lancaster.

The Wall – a huge wall, built in the north, to keep the barbarians at bay. Hadrian's Wall, anyone?

Iron Islands – the Ironborn's distinctive culture of maritime raiding mimics that of the Vikings.

Dothraki – the ancient Scythians, Huns and Mongols all resemble the Dothraki: fierce, horseback warriors from the grasslands.

Unsullied – the elite eunuch slave army suggests two formidable historical fighting forces. The Janissaries of the Ottoman Empire were recruited from Christian youths in the Balkans who were converted to Islam and trained for military service. The Mamluks of medieval Egypt were originally slave soldiers, but they took control and established a Middle Eastern dynasty.

Red Wedding – two events from Scottish history recall this bloody betrayal of the Stark family. The Black Dinner of 1440 witnessed the murder of the 16-year-old Earl of Douglas and his younger brother after being invited to dine at Edinburgh Castle with the boy king James II. In the Massacre of Glencoe in 1692 the laws of hospitality were shredded once again. Soldiers under Archibald Campbell, 10th Earl of Argyll, had arrived at Glencoe seeking shelter and were billeted by the MacDonald clan, honouring the Highland hospitality code. After a week with no hint of what was to come, the armed guests turned on the MacDonalds, murdering 38 members of the family.

Daenerys Targaryen – her life in exile, rise to power and return to seize the throne of her homeland resemble the career of Henry Tudor. He became King Henry VII in 1485 after defeating Richard III at the Battle of Bosworth. The only dragon he had was the red one on his banners.

INCREDIBLE SHRINKING LAKES

Great bodies of water that are rapidly disappearing.

Aral Sea, Kazakhstan and Uzbekistan – Central Asian lake that was once the world's fourth largest inland body of water. In the 1950s the Soviet authorities diverted water from the two main rivers that fed the lake for desert irrigation projects. The effect was disastrous and the Aral Sea began to shrink. By 1990 it had split into two separate parts, with dramatically increased salinity levels in what remained. Environmental degradation continued and within 40 years it had lost almost 90% of its surface area.

Lake Chad, Chad, Cameroon, Niger and Nigeria – once the world's sixth largest lake, it provides water for up to 30 million people in the surrounding African countries. Drought and the removal of water for irrigation and industry have led to a catastrophic reduction. Already a very shallow lake, it is now barely 10% of its earlier size.

Lake Urmia, Iran – formerly the largest lake in the Middle East and the sixth largest salt lake in the world, it has lost 95% of its water over the past 20 years.

Lake Poopó, Bolivia – large saline lake in the Altiplano Mountains. El Niño, climate change and the appropriation of water have meant that losses from evaporation have not been replenished. By 2016, the lake had virtually disappeared.

——— JINGLES RINGING BELLS ———

Modern advertising slogans and taglines that have entered the vernacular.

1000 songs in your pocket – **iPod**

Because you're worth it – **L'Oréal**

Chuck out your chintz – **IKEA**

Eat fresh – **Subway**

Finger lickin' good – **KFC**

Have a break… have a Kit Kat – **Kit Kat**

Hello boys – **Wonderbra**

For everything else, there's Mastercard – **Mastercard**

I'll slip an extra shrimp on the barbie – **Australia tourism campaign**

I'm lovin' it – **McDonald's**

It could be you – **UK National Lottery**

It does exactly what it says on the tin – **Ronseal**

It gives you wings – **Red Bull**

Just do it – **Nike**

Love it or hate it – **Marmite**

Maybe she's born with it. Maybe it's Maybelline – **Maybelline cosmetics**

Never knowingly undersold – **John Lewis**

Probably the best lager in the world – **Carlsberg**

Real beauty – **Dove skincare**

Refreshes the parts other beers cannot reach – **Heineken**

Simples – **Compare the Market (or Meerkat)**

The best a man can get – **Gillette razors**

The future's bright, the future's orange – **Orange telecommunications**

The mint with the hole – **Polo mints**

Think different – **Apple computers**

Va Va Voom – **Renault**

Vorsprung durch Technik – **Audi**

Where do you want to go today? – **Microsoft**

———— DO YOU WANT FREEDOM FRIES WITH THAT? ————

Foods and other things rebranded in the name of politics and patriotism.

Cities – on the outbreak of the First World War, the name of the Russian capital was changed from St Petersburg to the less Germanic-sounding Petrograd. In America, a number of towns and small communities called Berlin also changed their names.

Diseases – in 1918 it became impossible for an American infant to catch German measles; it would suffer from liberty measles instead.

Dogs – anti-German sentiment even extended to animals. Dachshunds, already unpopular as the Kaiser's favourite pets, were alternatively called badger dogs or liberty pups. After the First World War the UK Kennel Club officially renamed the German shepherd breed as the Alsatian, a designation that lasted until 1977.

Food – after the USA entered the First World War, growing anti-German feeling led to sauerkraut becoming liberty cabbage on menus, while hamburgers were liberty sandwiches. In the 1960s, when Communist China was perceived as a threat, the Chinese gooseberry was rebranded as the Kiwi fruit. In 2003, France's reluctance to support the invasion of Iraq led to a renaming of French fries as freedom fries in cafeterias at the US Congress.

Royal family – in 1917, King George V changed the name of the British royal family from Saxe-Coburg and Gotha to the more English-sounding Windsor.

Sports teams – in 1953, at the height of anti-Communist hysteria in the USA, the baseball team the Cincinnati Reds changed their name to the Redlegs.

DADDY, WHAT DID YOU DO IN THE GREAT EDIT WAR?

There are over five and half million articles on Wikipedia's English language pages. The site's plea that "editors should treat each other with respect and civility" can get lost in the midst of an edit war. Often the more trivial the discussion the more heated the debate.

MOST EDITED ARTICLES ON WIKIPEDIA

List of WWE personnel
George W. Bush
United States
Wikipedia
Jesus
Michael Jackson
Catholic Church

Barack Obama
List of programmes broadcast
   by ABS-CBN
     (Philippines TV network)
Adolf Hitler
Donald Trump

EDITS THAT TURNED NASTY

Jimmy Wales' birthdate – should the founder of Wikipedia be allowed, as he did in 2007, to remove the details of his birthdate from the site?

Frédéric Chopin – was the composer Polish, French, French-Polish or Polish-French? And shouldn't that first name be Fryderyk?

Ukraine's capital city – should it be rendered Kyiv or Kiev in English? The latter is the usual transliteration from Russian but it is better known internationally than the Ukrainian version.

Arachnophobia – should this article be illustrated with a picture of a spider?

Death Star – Luke Skywalker thought it was the size of a "small moon". But how big was it exactly?

Chicken, Alaska – how much demographic data is actually needed for an article on a town with at most 17 residents? Plus some assorted poultry, presumably.

Europe – is it even a continent in its own right, or just the western end of the vast Eurasian land mass?

The Pope – Supreme Pontiff or just Bishop of Rome?

Lady Jane Grey – was the "Nine Days' Queen" of 1553 actually a queen at all?

THE WORLD OF 2030: 8 AND A HALF BILLION PEOPLE, LIVING IN MEGACITIES

More than half the world's population now lives in cities. The trend towards urbanisation is accelerating and by 2030, according to United Nations predictions, these will be the 15 largest megacities.

City	Country	Population (million)
Tokyo	Japan	37.1
Delhi	India	36
Shanghai	China	30.7
Mumbai	India	27.7
Beijing	China	27.7
Dhaka	Bangladesh	27.3
Karachi	Pakistan	24.8
Cairo	Egypt	24.5
Lagos	Nigeria	24.2
Mexico City	Mexico	23.8
São Paulo	Brazil	23.4
Kinshasa	DR Congo	19.9
Osaka	Japan	19.9
New York	USA	19.8
Kolkata	India	19.0

———— THEY'VE AN AWFUL LOT OF COFFEE IN BRAZIL ————

And quite a bit of tea in China, too. These are the leading producers of some of our favourite pick-me-ups.

Coffee – Brazil produces 51 million 60kg bags (32% of world production).

Tea – China grows 2.4 million tonnes (over 40% of global total).

Sugar – Brazil produces 39 million tonnes of sugar (over 20% of world output).

Cocoa – Ivory Coast harvests 1.8 million tonnes (around a third of world total).

—————— BURSTING BUBBLES ——————

What goes up must come down, and boom is invariably followed by bust. These are some of the most spectacular financial bubbles that popped with a bang.

Tulip mania – in 1630s Holland a frenzy of speculation surrounded the sale of tulip bulbs. The rising price of bulbs attracted investors and a futures market was created in tulip contracts. The crash came when doubts emerged over the sustainability of the sky-high prices. The first recorded asset bubble had burst, leaving financial ruin in its wake.

South Sea bubble – the South Sea Company was founded in 1711 to trade, mostly in slaves, with South America once the War of the Spanish Succession had ended. King George I became a governor and the company began to deal in the national debt. Its share price rocketed on the rumours of the lucrative potential of the New World trade. When confidence collapsed in 1720 it lost more than 90% of its value and threatened to wreck the British financial system. Isaac Newton, himself a major investor in South Sea stock, reportedly said "I can calculate the movement of the stars, but not the madness of men".

Railway mania – the dot-com boom of its day. The right to build and operate railways in Britain was granted to companies by Parliament. The railway mania reached its peak in 1846 when there were 272 Acts authorising over 9,000 miles of new routes. The rise in railway shares encouraged fevered speculation, but overexpansion and poor economic conditions meant that around a third of the projects were never completed.

Wall Street Crash – the US stock market collapse in 1929 signalled the end of the Roaring Twenties and ushered in the Great Depression.

Dot-com bubble – the potential profits to be made on the Internet encouraged a speculative rise in share prices in the years before 2000. The promise of the "dot-com" companies was to shatter old orthodoxies and do business in a new way. Unfortunately, few were actually making money and once the start-up capital had been exhausted, doubts set in. Stock markets that had risen rapidly on expectations of a future bonanza came back to earth with a bump.

Global financial crisis – this started with the 2007 crisis in the American housing market. Subprime mortgage lending had inflated the housing bubble but when default rates began to rise, contagion spread through the international financial system. The Northern Rock building society was nationalised in the UK; Lehman Brothers bank collapsed in the US. And that was just the beginning of the chaos.

HOW TALL IS THAT TREE?

It's a question we've all asked ourselves. Here are three ways to get an answer.

Shadow – On a sunny day, stand by the tree you want to measure. Measure the full length of your shadow. Then, before the Sun has time to change position, measure the tree's shadow length. Divide the length of the tree's shadow by the length of your shadow. And multiply this total by your actual height. The result is the height of the tree.

Pencil – Get a friend to stand by the tree you want to measure. Position yourself where you can see the top of the tree and hold out a pencil at arm's length. Close one eye and move the pencil so that the tip aligns with the top of the tree. Get your thumbnail to match up with the very bottom of the tree. So now the whole height of the tree is "behind" the pencil. Rotate your arm so the pencil is horizontal i.e. parallel to the ground. Get your friend to move about until they are in line with the top of the pencil. Measure how far they are from the base of the tree. And this will give you the height of the tree.

Paper triangle – Fold a square piece of paper in half to create a right-angled triangle (with two other angles of 45 degrees each). Hold the triangle up to your face so that the right angle is away from you and you're looking up and along the hypotenuse (longest side). Close one eye, look up and move backwards until the top of the tree is aligned with the top of the triangle. Then measure the distance from you to the tree. Add your height to this figure. And now you have the height of the tree.

——————— **MODERN MINDS: SIX OF THE BEST** ———————

A very brief introduction to some of the most influential living thinkers.

Noam Chomsky – theoretical linguist who proposed the revolutionary, and still controversial, idea that the human ability to learn languages is partly innate. He famously illustrated the difference between syntax and semantics with "colourless green ideas sleep furiously", a sentence that is grammatically correct, but meaningless. Since the Vietnam War he has been a prominent critic of American foreign policy.

Judith Butler – American philosopher who revolutionised gender theory. In her bestselling book *Gender Trouble* (1990) she argued that gender is socially constructed rather than intrinsic i.e. people "learn" to be men and women, and gender is formed by repeated performance of a role. Heteronormative ideas of sexuality are a way of enforcing the status quo in which women are dominated by men while gay and trans people are marginalised. Her work expands on the idea of the earlier feminist icon Simone de Beauvoir that "one is not born, but rather becomes, a woman".

Slavoj Žižek – Slovenian cultural theorist. Intellectually playful and provocative, Žižek's work combines psychoanalysis, philosophy and politics across a dizzying range of subjects. He is equally at home discussing Marxism (he still claims to be a Communist), the ethics of Keanu Reeves in *Speed* and the philosophical significance of Viagra. Žižek has been dubbed both the "Elvis of cultural theory" and the "most dangerous philosopher in the West".

Thomas Nagel – philosopher, whose work examines the contradiction between our personal, subjective view of events and ideas and the apparent objective realities of the world. How do we know anything or understand minds other than our own? His most renowned work is the 1974 paper "What is it Like to be a Bat?". In this thought experiment Nagel suggested that while a human could imagine hanging upside down, eating insects and navigating by echolocation, we still wouldn't know what it is like to "be" a bat.

Cornel West – philosopher and social critic, perhaps the most prominent African-American intellectual working today. His best-known work, the book of essays *Race Matters* (1993), was given a timely reissue in 2018 in the era of the #blacklivesmatter movement and the events of Baltimore, Ferguson, and Charlottesville.

Peter Singer – Australian philosopher, whose work laid the foundations for the modern animal rights movement. His book *Animal Liberation* (1976) argued that human abuse of animals in laboratories and factory farms was morally indefensible.

NO ONE LEFT TO TALK TO?

According to UNESCO, there are over 200 languages across the world with ten or fewer speakers. Another 200+ languages have become extinct in the past century. Threatened languages are divided into one of five categories:

Vulnerable – most children speak the language, but it may be restricted to certain places (e.g. in the home). Examples include Basque, Bavarian, Belarusian, Faroese and Welsh.

Definitely endangered – children no longer learn the language as a "mother tongue" in the home. Includes Irish, Scottish Gaelic, Yiddish and Romani.

Severely endangered – language is spoken by grandparents and the older generations. While the parent generation may understand it, they do not speak it to children or among themselves. Includes Breton, Guernsey and Jersey French, Burgundian and North Frisian.

Critically endangered – the youngest speakers are grandparents and older, and they speak the language partially and infrequently. Examples include Cornish and Manx.

Extinct – there are no speakers left. Includes Alderney French from the Channel Islands.

---------------- **MAKING A MEAL OF IT** ----------------

A menu of eponymous foods.

PRE-DINNER COCKTAILS

Bellini – mixture of Prosecco sparkling wine and peach purée, named after the 15th-century Venetian painter Giovanni Bellini.

Shirley Temple – sickly sweet mix of ginger ale and grenadine, named for the equally sickly-sweet child actress. She hated the drink, apparently.

SNACKS AND STARTERS

Carpaccio – dish of thinly sliced raw meat, named after another Venetian Renaissance artist.

Nachos – its origin is disputed, but the strongest claim is that of the Mexican chef Ignacio (Nacho) Anaya, who worked in a town near the US border in the 1940s.

Sandwich – named after the 18th-century aristocrat, John Montagu, the 4th Earl of Sandwich. An inveterate gambler, he would eat the snack while playing at the card tables.

MAINS

Chateaubriand steak – thick beef fillet steak, named after the author and diplomat François-René, Vicomte de Chateaubriand, one of the pioneers of French Romanticism.

Tournedos Rossini – another steak dish, this time topped by a slice of foie gras and garnished with truffle. Created in honour of the Italian operatic composer and renowned gourmand Giacomo Rossini.

Beef Wellington – thought to be named after the victor of Waterloo, its origins can't be traced back further than the early 20th century.

Omelette Arnold Bennett – created at the Savoy hotel for the author of *Anna of the Five Towns*, it combined haddock, cream and Parmesan.

Margherita pizza – although disputed by some food historians, the quintessential pizza is claimed to be named after Margherita of Savoy, queen of post-unification Italy.

CAKES AND DESSERTS

Victoria sponge – the invention of baking powder in the 1840s allowed cakes to rise higher than before. Named after Britain's queen, the first recorded recipe for the Victoria sandwich is from 1861 in *Mrs Beeton's Book of Household Management*.

Kaiserschmarrn – a dessert of sweet shredded pancakes, said to take its name from Emperor Franz Josef I of Austria.

Peach Melba – a dish of peaches and ice cream, served with raspberry sauce. It was created by the French chef Auguste Escoffier to honour the Australian soprano Nellie Melba. He also devised Melba toast for her.

THE REAL TWITTERATI

The RSPB's annual Big Garden Birdwatch is the UK's biggest citizen science survey. In January 2018, 420,489 people across the country counted a total of 6,764,475 birds. These are the ten most common garden birds.

1. House sparrow
2. Starling
3. Blue tit
4. Blackbird
5. Wood pigeon
6. Goldfinch
7. Great tit
8. Robin
9. Long-tailed tit
10. Chaffinch

Although the sparrow is still the most common garden bird in Britain, its numbers have decreased alarmingly in the past 25 years. A more than 50% decline in its breeding population has earned it a place on the Birds of Conservation Concern red list.

UNSOLVED MYSTERIES OF SCIENCE

Ten problems that the biggest brains are still wrangling with.

What happened before the Big Bang?
Around 13.8 billion years ago, the universe is thought to have emerged from a point of seemingly infinite density and temperature. What preceded this?

What is the universe actually made of?
Scientists estimate that everything we can observe in the universe (planets, stars, galaxies etc.) only represents about 5% of the total stuff out there. So what accounts for the other 95%? The most widely accepted cosmological model suggests around 68% of the universe is mysterious "dark energy" and the remaining 27% is "dark matter".

How did life evolve?
Earth is around 4.5 billion years old. While the first fossils date back to 3.5 billion years ago, there is evidence of life almost 500 million years before this.

Why does time only flow in one direction?
It's hypothesised that the one-way arrow of time is connected with entropy and the second law of thermodynamics.

Is there intelligent life elsewhere in the universe?
Assuming that there's some here, of course. Fermi's paradox is the supposed contradiction between the probability of alien life existing and the lack of evidence for it. In short, where is everybody?

How will the universe end?
With a bang, a whimper, or more probably, a "Big Crunch" in which the expansion of space starts to reverse.

Is ours the only universe?
The once-fantastical idea of the "multiverse" is gaining acceptance among scientists.

What is consciousness?
How does a mass of nerve cells create our thoughts, memories and emotions?

Can computers replicate the human mind?
In 1951, Alan Turing proposed a test for machine intelligence called the Imitation Game. More recently, Microsoft's AI chatbot Tay was shut down 16 hours after its launch when it posted abusive messages on Twitter, caused by trolls who instigated inflammatory interactions so that Tay would respond in kind. So there is some way to go.

Why do we dream?
Sigmund Freud thought that dreams revealed our unconscious desires; it usually boiled down to sex. No surprises there. But even now neuroscientists can't agree on the form and function of dreams.

WHAT ARE WE MADE OF?

The human body, broken down into its constituent chemical elements. Almost 99% of the body's mass is made up of just six elements.

Element	% by mass	Mass (kg, in 75kg person)
Oxygen	65	48.75
Carbon	18	13.5
Hydrogen	10	7.5
Nitrogen	3	2.25
Calcium	1.5	1.125
Phosphorus	1	0.75
Potassium	0.35	0.26
Sulphur	0.25	0.1875
Others	0.9	0.675

That's well over 40 litres of water and enough phosphorus to make 2,200 match heads, iron to make a 7cm nail and carbon for 900 pencils.

--- **ART ATTACK!** ---

Modern artworks that shocked the world.

Les Demoiselles d'Avignon by Pablo Picasso, 1907. Picasso's primitive angular portrayal of five nude prostitutes shocked even his friends in the art world. The painting wasn't shown publicly until 1916. Now it is considered a key work in the development of Cubism and modern art.

Fountain by Marcel Duchamp, 1917. A porcelain urinal, signed with the name "R. Mutt". It is the best known of his "ready-made" works, which raised commonplace, mass-produced objects to the level of art. Duchamp submitted it to a New York show in 1917, but the organisers refused to exhibit it on the grounds that it was in no sense a work of art.

Equivalent VIII by Carl Andre, 1966. 120 bricks, arranged in a rectangle. The work caused an outcry after it was purchased by the Tate Gallery, the tabloid press arguing that it was a waste of public money.

Piss Christ by Andres Serrano, 1987. A photograph depicting a crucifix submerged in the artist's own urine. It was denounced by Christian conservatives in the US and provoked a debate over state funding of the arts.

The Physical Impossibility of Death in the Mind of Someone Living by Damien Hirst, 1991. A 14-foot tiger shark preserved in formaldehyde. The cost of the work was met by the advertising executive Charles Saatchi, a keen collector of modern art. Hirst followed this up with works involving a preserved sheep (*Away from the Flock*) and cows (*Mother and Child, Divided*). After winning the Turner Prize in 1995, he said: "It's amazing what you can do with an E in A-level art, twisted imagination and a chainsaw."

Myra by Marcus Harvey, 1995. A giant portrait of the murderer Myra Hindley, made from child-sized handprints. It was a controversial inclusion in the Sensation exhibition of Young British Artists at the Royal Academy of Art in 1997.

Everyone I Have Ever Slept With 1963–1995 by Tracey Emin, 1995. A tent embroidered with the names of the 102 people that the artist had (literally) slept with since her birth. It was destroyed in 2004 in a fire at a storage warehouse.

───── TRACTOR BOYS, HONEST MEN AND AN OLD LADY ─────

An A–Z of football's more colourful team nicknames.

Alemannia Aachen (Germany) .... Potato Beetles
Ayr United .... Honest Men
Benevento (Italy) .... Witches
Chievo (Italy) .... Flying Donkeys
Cowdenbeath .... Blue Brazil
Dundee United .... Tangerines
Estudiantes (Argentina) .... Rat Stabbers
Everton .... Toffees
Fulham .... Cottagers
Grimsby Town .... Mariners
Hartlepool .... Monkey Hangers
Heart of Midlothian .... Jam Tarts
Ipswich Town .... Tractor Boys
Juventus (Italy) .... the Old Lady
Kidderminster Harriers .... Carpetmen
Leicester City .... Foxes
Málaga (Spain) .... Anchovies
Manchester United .... Red Devils
Newell's Old Boys (Argentina) .... Lepers
Northampton Town .... Cobblers
Oldham Athletic .... Latics
Partick Thistle .... Jags
Peterborough United .... Posh
Queen's Park .... Spiders
Rosenborg (Norway) .... Troll Children
Sheffield United .... Blades
Tottenham Hotspur .... Lilywhites
Udinese (Italy) .... Little Zebras
Villareal .... Yellow Submarine
West Bromwich Albion .... Baggies
Xelajú MC (Guatemala) .... Super Goats
York City .... Minstermen
Zamalek SC (Egypt) .... White Castle

---------------------- **DEM BONES** ----------------------

The posthumous history of some famous body parts.

Walter Raleigh's head – after his execution for treason in 1618, Walter Raleigh's wife Elizabeth took his severed head away with her. She is said to have had it embalmed and carried it around in a red velvet bag for the rest of her life.

St Francis Xavier's toe – the missionary saint who preached Catholicism across Asia died en route to China in 1552. When his uncorrupted corpse was later displayed in Goa, India, an overenthusiastic worshipper bit off his big toe.

Oliver Cromwell's head – the Lord Protector of the English Commonwealth died in 1658. Two years later, with the monarchy restored under Charles II, his body was exhumed, hanged at Tyburn and his head placed on a spike at Westminster Hall. For almost 30 years it remained until it was dislodged in a gale. Thereafter its history is murky. What is claimed to be Cromwell's head passed through the hands of collectors and was intermittently put on public display. Historians and scientists debated its authenticity until finally the relic was buried in 1960 in the chapel of Cromwell's old Cambridge college, Sidney Sussex.

Napoleon's penis – it was claimed to have been removed during his autopsy in 1821 on the island of St Helena. As part of a collection of Napoleonic relics bought by a London book dealer in 1916 it was listed coyly as "mummified tendon". In 1977 it was acquired by a New Jersey urologist and remains in the possession of his family. Size-wise, it is said to be nothing special and resembles a shrivelled eel.

Thomas Hardy's heart – the funeral of the writer Thomas Hardy in 1928 united Britain's literary and political establishment; his pall-bearers at Westminster Abbey included Prime Minister Stanley Baldwin, Leader of the Opposition Ramsay MacDonald, Rudyard Kipling, George Bernard Shaw and J.M. Barrie. His heart was not there, however, as it had been removed after death to be buried in his native Dorset. According to a persistent rumour, the doctor left the organ unattended and returned to find a cat eating it.

Einstein's brain – following his death in 1955, it was taken away and kept by the pathologist Thomas Harvey. He hoped that studying it would provide insights into the nature of genius. Examination of the brain in the intervening years suggests that physiology alone will not provide an answer to this.

Mussolini's blood – in 2009, some of the Italian fascist leader's blood and parts of his brain were listed for sale on the auction website eBay. They were removed after protests from his MP granddaughter Alessandra.

Tchaikowsky's skull – when he died in 1982 the Polish pianist and composer André Tchaikowsky bequeathed his skull to the Royal Shakespeare Company. He wanted it to be used as an authentic prop in productions of Hamlet. He got his posthumous wish in 2009 and it was even featured on the Royal Mail stamp depicting David Tennant's Hamlet holding Yorick's skull aloft.

———————— TIME ON YOUR HANDS ————————

1,000,000 nanoseconds	1 millisecond
1,000 milliseconds	1 second
60 seconds	1 minute
60 minutes	1 hour
24 hours	1 day
7 days	1 week
52 weeks and 1 day	1 ordinary year
365 days, 5 hours, 48 minutes 46 seconds	1 solar year
366 days	1 leap year

When the Gregorian calendar was introduced in 1582, the 4th October was followed immediately by the 15th October; the ten days in between simply disappeared for that year! Britain waited until 1752 before adopting the new calendar, this time missing out 3rd to 13th September.

In 2018, Facebook announced that one of their engineers had invented a new unit of time called the Flick (from frame-tick). Defined as 1/705,600,000 of a second (a bit larger than a nanosecond) it exactly subdivides media frame rates thus helping to keep video effects in sync.

I BET YOU THINK THIS SONG IS ABOUT YOU

The inspirations behind some well-known works.

Carole King – the prolific and wildly successful songwriter was herself the inspiration for a major hit, Neil Sedaka's 1959 song "Oh! Carol". They had been an item in high school in New York.

Helô Pinheiro – the 17-year-old's daily walk to the beach in Rio de Janeiro moved Antônio Carlos Jobim and Vinicius de Moraes to write the bossa nova classic "The Girl from Ipanema" in 1962.

Warren Beatty (or perhaps Dan Armstrong) or possibly Mick Jagger, David Geffen or David Bowie. They're all candidates for the inspiration of Carly Simon's "You're So Vain". At a charity auction in 2003, the head of NBC Sports paid $50,000 to hear from Simon herself who the song was about. But he was sworn to secrecy and the mystery endured.

Pattie Boyd – a leading model in the 1960s who became the wife and muse of George Harrison and later Eric Clapton. She inspired some of their greatest songs: Harrison's "If I Needed Someone", "For You Blue" and "Something" as well as Clapton's "Layla" and "Wonderful Tonight".

Linda McCartney – Paul McCartney didn't hide his love away for his wife Linda, writing numerous songs about her. They include "Two of Us", "The Lovely Linda" and, most memorably, "Maybe I'm Amazed".

Maxine Feibelman – she was the "seamstress for the band" who married Elton John's lyricist Bernie Taupin and inspired the song "Tiny Dancer".

Billie Jean King – Elton John wrote the song "Philadelphia Freedom" for the tennis star who was part of the Philadelphia Freedoms professional team.

Carrie Fisher – Paul Simon wrote "Hearts and Bones" about his relationship with the *Star Wars* actress, whom he had married in 1983.

Rosanna Arquette – she provided the title of the hit "Rosanna" by Toto; she was dating the keyboardist at the time. It's also claimed she inspired "In Your Eyes" by Peter Gabriel, with whom she had a relationship in the 1980s.

Britney Spears – "Cry Me a River" articulated Justin Timberlake's struggle to come to terms with the end of his relationship with fellow pop star and *Mickey Mouse Club* alumna Britney Spears.

John Mayer – Taylor Swift's "Dear John" is another break-up song, thought to refer to her split with the singer Mayer.

——— FUN WITH FLAGS ———

Parrots, guns and other unusual objects found on flags.

Angola .... machete and cogged wheel
Bermuda .... sinking ship
Cambodia .... Angkor Wat temple
Cyprus .... map outline of the country
Dominica .... parrot
Ecuador .... condor and Mount Chimborazo
Falkland Islands .... sheep
Fiji .... cocoa pod, sugar cane and a bunch of bananas
Guam .... coconut tree
Kenya and Swaziland .... spears and shield
Kiribati .... frigatebird
Mexico ..... eagle, grasping a snake, standing on a prickly pear cactus
Mozambique .... AK-47 assault rifle with bayonet attached
Nepal .... world's only national flag that is not a quadrilateral
Papua New Guinea .... Raggiana bird of paradise
Peru .... vicuña, a relative of the llama
Saudi Arabia .... sword and shahada (Islamic declaration of faith)
Turkmenistan .... five carpet designs
Uganda .... grey crowned crane
Wales and Bhutan .... dragons

—————— HASTINGS, AGINCOURT... AIN JALUT? ——————

Decisive battles you might not know about but probably should.

Talas, AD 751 – fought between the forces of the Chinese T'ang Empire and Arabs of the Abbasid Caliphate, it is thought to have taken place on the border of modern-day Kazakhstan and Kyrgyzstan. It led to the end of Buddhism in Central Asia, as the region passed into the Muslim sphere of influence. Chinese captives are believed to have introduced paper-making to the city of Samarkand; the great secret was out. Talas was the only major battle between the armies of China and medieval Islam.

Manzikert, 1071 – a key event in the history of Europe and the Near East. The army of Byzantine Emperor Romanus IV Diogenes met the Seljuks north of Lake Van, in what is now eastern Turkey. The battle was a disaster for the Byzantines; Romanus was captured and territory was ceded to the Turks. It marked the start of their westward march into the Byzantine heartland of Anatolia. The First Crusade has its origins in the subsequent Byzantine appeals for help from fellow Christians in Western Europe.

Bouvines, 1214 – fought southwest of Lille, near the modern Franco-Belgian border. King of France Philip II Augustus defeated the combined forces of the Holy Roman Emperor Otto IV, the Rhineland princes and King John of England. The French victory cemented John's loss of Normandy and set him on the path to civil war that ended with the humiliation of Magna Carta in 1215. The French monarchy emerged with enhanced prestige and power.

Ain Jalut, 1260 – the seemingly unstoppable march of the Mongols was halted at Ain Jalut, in Galilee in modern Israel. They were defeated by an army of Mamluks, the former slave soldiers who had taken power in Egypt. The Mongols suffered their first major defeat and Mamluk rule survived in Egypt and Syria until the 16th century.

Lepanto, 1571 – the largest sea battle ever fought in the Mediterranean, it pitched the Ottoman Turks against the Holy League of Venice, Habsburg Spain, Malta and an Italian papal alliance. It took place in the Gulf of Patras in the Ionian Sea. The rout of the Ottoman fleet was the first major Christian naval victory over the Turks and halted their westward expansion. Lepanto was also the last great battle between war galleys. Author of *Don Quixote*, Miguel de Cervantes, lost the use of his left arm in the fighting.

Imphal, 1944 – fought around the capital of Manipur state in north-eastern India. An Anglo-Indian force stopped the advance of the Japanese, inflicting heavy casualties amid fierce fighting. It was an unprecedented military defeat for Japan and saved India from the threat of invasion.

Cuito Cuanavale, 1987–8 – the biggest battle fought in Africa since Rommel's defeat at El Alamein in 1942. South Africa and the UNITA rebels clashed with the Angolan army and its Cuban and Namibian allies around a military airfield in southern Angola. Both sides claimed victory, but South Africa was no longer able to stand in the way of Namibian independence or delay reform at home. In 1991 Nelson Mandela thanked Fidel Castro for his support, saying "the decisive defeat of the aggressive apartheid forces destroyed the myth of the invincibility of the white oppressor".

——————— IT'S THE ECONOMY, STUPID ———————

The global economy is worth around \$74 trillion, according to the World Bank. The world's top ten economies account for around two-thirds of this.

Value of economy	Country	Global share %
\$18 trillion	USA	24.3
\$11 trillion	China	14.8
\$4.4 trillion	Japan	5.9
\$3.3 trillion	Germany	4.5
\$2.9 trillion	UK	3.9
\$2.4 trillion	France	3.3
\$2 trillion	India	2.8
\$1.8 trillion	Italy	2.5
\$1.8 trillion	Brazil	2.4
\$1.5 trillion	Canada	2.1

—————— YOU SAY YOU WANT A REVOLUTION ——————

Since the 1970s, revolutions and popular uprisings have been given some colourful names.

Carnation Revolution Portugal, 1974 – A bloodless military coup, coupled with wider social protest led to the collapse of the dictatorship and independence for Portugal's African colonies. The revolution got its popular name from the flowers placed in the muzzles of tanks and guns.

People Power (or Yellow) Revolution Philippines, 1986 – Yellow ribbon-wearing protesters took to the streets after the murder of former senator Benigno Aquino at Manila airport. His widow Corazon led the movement that overthrew the dictatorship of President Ferdinand Marcos. She replaced him as president, helping to establish a democratic Philippines.

Velvet Revolution Czechoslovakia, 1989 – The non-violent end of Communist power was followed three years later by a similarly peaceful Velvet Divorce as the country split into the Czech Republic and Slovakia.

Bulldozer Revolution Yugoslavia, 2000 – The ousting of President Slobodan Milosevic, who died five years later while on trial for war crimes at The Hague.

Rose Revolution Georgia, 2003 – The first of the so-called "colour" revolutions in the former Soviet Union. President Eduard Shevardnadze retired in the face of protests led by his eventual successor Mikheil Saakashvili. He and his supporters had forced their way into the Georgian parliament clutching red roses and calling on Shevardnadze to resign.

Orange Revolution Ukraine, 2004 – Political upheaval and mass protests after the contentious victory of Viktor Yanukovych in a presidential election run-off. Under intense international scrutiny the election was re-run and his opponent Viktor Yushchenko declared the winner. Ten years later civil unrest erupted again in the more violent Euromaidan stand-off in Kiev.

Tulip Revolution Kyrgyzstan, 2005 – Protesters, many on horseback, took to the streets after a disputed parliamentary election. It led to the resignation of Kyrgyz President Askar Akayev.

Cedar Revolution Lebanon, 2005 – Peaceful rallies following the assassination of former prime minister Rafik Hariri. Demonstrators demanded the removal of Syrian troops in Lebanon and an end to Syrian interference in Lebanese politics.

Jeans Revolution Belarus, 2006 – Protesters wore denim, once a symbol of the West, to demonstrate against the re-election of President Alexander Lukashenko. His regime has long been described as Europe's last dictatorship.

Jasmine Revolution Tunisia, 2010 – The Arab Spring began with the self-immolation of street vendor Mohamed Bouazizi, driven to despair over his treatment by local officials. The protests spread in scale and scope, eventually leading to the overthrow of President Zine El Abidine Ben Ali. The term "Jasmine Revolution", though common in Western media reporting, was not widely used in Tunisia itself.

WILDLIFE ON THE BRINK

These are the world's most endangered mammals, according to the WWF.

Amur leopard
Bornean orangutan
Sumatran orangutan
Tapanuli orangutan
Sumatran elephant
Cross River gorilla
Eastern lowland gorilla
Western lowland gorilla
Mountain gorilla
Black rhino

Javan rhino
Sumatran rhino
Saola (horned bovine in the forests of Laos and Vietnam)
South China tiger
Malayan tiger
Sumatran tiger
Vaquita (porpoise, native to the Gulf of California)
Yangtze finless porpoise

PHISH AND CHIPS

It's no longer a West African prince with a fortune that he's just itching to share with you. Online scams are getting more prevalent and more devious.

Phishing – an email purportedly from a bank, financial institution or government agency encourages you to click on a link or attachment. This will install malware and give the hacker access to personal information on your computer. Or the message directs you to a fake website where your password and other confidential details will be harvested by the fraudsters. An attempt to gain this information by phone is known as "vishing". And by text message it's "smishing".

419 scams – you're contacted out of the blue by someone asking you to pay a fee to move money from one country to another. You'll be in line for a generous cut once the money is available. This scam, a type of advance fee fraud, is named after an article in the criminal code of Nigeria, where many of these schemes originate.

Authorised push-payment scam – fraudsters contact you posing as a business that you already owe money to. Your payment goes to the scammer's account rather than to the intended recipient. This is a growing area of fraud, facilitated by the instant transfer of money via online banking.

Lottery or competition scams – an email from an overseas lottery informs you that you're a winner. Just enter your personal details or ring a premium rate number to get your prize.

Dating and romance scams – fake profiles on dating sites are used to establish online relationships. Once trust is gained, a demand for money will arrive because of family illness, an accident or other "emergency".

Online shopping scams – products, often electronics, are offered for sale at knock-down prices. The goods you are actually sent are counterfeit or faulty, if anything arrives at all.

Scareware – a message pops up that your computer has been infected by a virus. It hasn't, but the fake anti-virus software offered as a remedy can disable your computer if downloaded.

———————— **HOW OLD ARE YOU REALLY?** ————————

Different parts of the body renew themselves at different rates.

Skin   The surface of the skin is replaced every two weeks.

Hair   Head hair grows on average 0.44mm per day. The individual hairs may be up to seven years old. Eyebrows regrow in around 60 days.

Nails   Fingernails grow around 3mm a month, more than twice as quickly as toenails. If you lose a fingernail, it will take 4–6 months to grow a replacement.

Brain   Cells in the cerebral cortex are not renewed; they're as old as you are. However, new neurons (brain cells) are developed in the hippocampus, even into old age.

Liver   The liver is the only internal organ that can naturally regenerate; it can recover its original mass even if up to 75% has been removed in surgery.

Eyes   Cells in the lens and retina do not renew themselves. The only part of the eye that does regenerate is the cornea.

Teeth   Tooth enamel is not replaced.

Bones   They are being continually renewed throughout the body. It takes around ten years for a complete human skeleton to be replaced.

Blood   Red blood cells only have a lifespan of around four months. Fortunately, they are constantly being produced in the bone marrow, along with white blood cells and platelets. The body's average daily blood cell production is around 200 billion red cells, 10 billion white cells and 400 billion platelets.

———————— WHERE DID EVERYBODY GO? ————————

What causes once-thriving towns and cities to lie empty and abandoned? In these examples it was earthquakes, volcanic eruptions, nuclear catastrophes, war and brutal economic realities.

Centralia, Pennsylvania – a fire in a coal mine beneath the town broke out in 1962. Attempts to extinguish the fire in the years that followed all failed and in 1980 a plan was drawn up to evacuate the town. It is now almost entirely deserted; the roads are cracked and sulphurous gases escape from fissures in the earth. And there's enough coal down there to keep the fire burning for another 200 years.

Craco, Italy – in 1963 a landslide, probably caused by infrastructure works, threatened this historic hillside town in southern Italy. Further natural disasters followed: a flood in 1972 and an earthquake in 1980, after which the town was finally evacuated. It was used as a location in the film *The Passion of the Christ*.

Hashima Island, Japan – undersea coal deposits explain why this 16-acre island became one of the most densely populated places in the world. At its peak in the 1950s more than 5,000 miners and their family members lived here, producing the coal that helped fuel the post-war Japanese economic miracle. By the early 1970s the mines were exhausted and the island was abandoned. It memorably featured in the James Bond film *Skyfall*.

Plymouth, Montserrat – a devastating volcanic eruption in 1997 buried the city under ash, causing its 4,000 inhabitants to flee. The southern half of the island is now an exclusion zone and a new capital is being developed to replaced Plymouth.

Pripyat, Ukraine – abandoned in 1986 on the day after the Chernobyl disaster, the world's worst nuclear accident. Pripyat once had a population of nearly 50,000 people. It had been founded in 1970 specifically to serve the very nuclear plant that later rendered it a ghost town. The Ferris wheel that still stands in the old amusement park has become an eerie symbol of the city.

Varosha, Cyprus – a suburb of Famagusta, lined with tourist hotels along the seafront. After the 1974 Turkish invasion of Cyprus it became a closed-off military zone and former residents were forbidden to return.

———————— THEY SAID IT FIRST ————————

Lexicographers at the *Oxford English Dictionary* have scoured the works of the great authors for the very first uses of words.

Geoffrey Chaucer (*c.*1342–1400)	1,957 words, including appearance, bagpipe, disarray, government, homecoming, impudence, misery, native, twitter, veal.
Christopher Marlowe (1564–1593)	122 words, including astounding, ceaseless, gloomy, musketeer, naturalized, pillage, radiance, scorched, squinting, unrelenting.
William Shakespeare (1564–1616)	1,483 words, including barefaced, critic, dangling, eventful, hunchbacked, investment, laughable, made-up, torturer, unearthly.
John Milton (1608–1674)	547 words, including awe-struck, depravity, enjoyable, exhilarating, fragrance, homogenous, irresponsible, mutter, pandemonium, stunning.
Samuel Pepys (1633–1703)	79 words, including envoy, frighten, gherkin, mantelpiece, nepotism, slide-rule, uninvited.
Walter Scott (1771–1832)	435 words, including berserk, captaincy, cold shoulder, freelance, hilarious, overcrowded, password, postponed, sporran, third party.
Jane Austen (1775–1817)	38 words, including door-bell, fragmented, irrepressible, outsider, sponge-cake, sympathizer.
Charles Dickens (1812–1870)	213 words, including abuzz, boredom, butter-fingers, confusingly, conspiratorial, fluffiness, flummox, manslaughter, messiness, rampage.

─────── BITING OFF LESS THAN WE CAN CHEW ───────

The modern weight-loss diet has its origins in William Banting's 1863 booklet *Letter on Corpulence Addressed to the Public*, in which he advised cutting back on sugar, starch, beer and butter. The appetite for fad diets and short-cuts to losing weight is seemingly endless. Here are some of the more recent diets that have caught the public imagination.

Scarsdale – a 1970s diet emphasising high protein intake at the expense of fat and carbohydrates. Its inventor Herman Tarnower named it after the town in New York state where he practised medicine. Three years after his bestselling *The Complete Scarsdale Medical Diet* was published he was shot dead by a former girlfriend.

F-plan – high-fibre and calorie control diet launched in 1982 by Audrey Eyton.

Atkins – a low-carbohydrate diet that was widely followed in the early 2000s. The initial stage aims for rapid weight loss via a protein-rich diet with very few carbohydrates. At the height of the diet's popularity in 2003, its creator Robert Atkins died after slipping on an icy pavement in New York.

South Beach – a low GI (glycaemic index) diet, originally developed in the 1990s by Florida cardiologist Arthur Agatston.

Cabbage soup or grapefruit – examples of fad diets that involve the heavy consumption of one type of food at virtually every meal. These crash diets rely on low calorie intakes that are unsustainable in the long run and the weight loss achieved usually proves temporary.

Paleo – eat like our hunter-gathering ancestors, in other words. Meat, fish, fruit, vegetables and seeds are allowed, but out go dairy products and grains. It aims to recreate the diet that preceded the development of farming around 10,000 years ago.

5:2 – a diet in which you eat normally for five days a week and fast on the other two.

--- **EUROZONE** ---

Introduced on 1 January 2002, the euro is now used by 340 million people.

Euro banknotes feature generic images of architectural styles from European history:

€5 .... Classical €100 .... Baroque and rococo
€10 .... Romanesque €200 .... 19th century iron and glass
€20 .... Gothic €500 .... 20th century modern
€50 .... Renaissance

Euro coins have a common side and a national side:
Andorra €1 .... Casa de la Vall, former seat of parliament
Austria €1 .... composer Wolfgang Amadeus Mozart
Belgium €1 .... King Philippe[1]
Cyprus €1 .... cruciform idol from 3000 BC
Estonia €1 .... country outline
Finland €1 .... flying swans
France €1 .... stylised tree
Germany €1 .... eagle
Greece €1 .... owl of Athena
Ireland €1 .... Celtic harp
Italy €1 .... Leonardo da Vinci's Vitruvian man drawing
Latvia €1 .... folk maiden
Lithuania €1 .... coat of arms of the republic
Luxembourg €1 .... Grand Duke Henri[2]
Malta €1 .... eight-pointed Maltese cross
Monaco €1 .... Prince Albert II[3]
Netherlands €1 (second series) .... King Willem-Alexander[4]
Portugal €1 .... royal seal of 1144
San Marino €1 (second series) .... 13th century Second Tower
Slovakia €1 .... double cross on three hills
Slovenia €1 .... writer Primož Trubar
Spain €1 .... King Felipe VI[5]
Vatican City €1 (fifth series) .... coat of arms of Pope Francis

Although they are not members of the European Union, the small states of Andorra, Monaco, San Marino, and the Vatican City are permitted to issue Euro coins. 1: reigned since 2013, 2: reigned since 2000, 3: reigned since 2005, 4: reigned since 2013, 5: reigned since 2014

—————— DEAD PARROTS AND OTHER EXTINCTIONS ——————

Some famous animal extinctions of the 20th and 21st centuries.

Huai – bird, native to New Zealand's North Island. Last recorded in 1907.

Passenger pigeon – once perhaps the world's most numerous bird, with an estimated North American population of 3 billion. Last wild passenger pigeon shot in 1900; last captive bird, named Martha, died in 1914 at Cincinnati Zoo.

Carolina parakeet – native to the eastern United States, ranging from Florida to Virginia. Last captive bird died in 1918.

Darwin's Galápagos mouse – found on the Galápagos Islands, but last seen in 1930. Probably driven to extinction by the introduction of the black rat to the islands.

Desert rat kangaroo – last confirmed sighting in 1935 in Southern Australia; unconfirmed night-time sighting in 2011, but presumed to be extinct.

Thylacine (Tasmanian tiger) – marsupial, once common across Australia. It suffered with the arrival of the dingo, and in the modern era it only survived in Tasmania. The last known Tasmanian tiger died in 1936 in Hobart Zoo.

Japanese sea lion – found in the northwest Pacific. The last confirmed sighting was of a small population in 1951 on Takeshima island.

Red-bellied gracile mouse opossum – only ever recorded in Argentina and last seen in 1962.

Kaua'i 'O'o – bird, native to Hawaii. Deforestation and the introduction of invasive species led to population collapse; by 1981 only a single pair remained. The last known surviving bird, a male, was sighted in 1985 and its mating call recorded in 1987.

Golden toad – once common in the high-altitude cloud forests of Costa Rica, it was last recorded in 1989. The toad is claimed to be the first species to have become extinct because of the effects of climate change.

Pinta giant tortoise – Lonesome George, the last known Pinta tortoise from the Galápagos Islands, died in 2012. He had been in captivity since 1972 and was estimated to be around 100 years old, relatively young for a giant tortoise! His preserved body is now on display at the American Museum of Natural History in New York.

———— SO GOOD THEY NAMED IT TWICE ————

Tautological place names from across the world.

River Avon – there are various rivers so named in Britain; Salisbury, Bristol and Shakespeare's Stratford all stand on different river Avons. The name derives from the Celtic word "abona", meaning river.

East Timor (Timor-Leste) – independent since 2002, following a bloody Indonesian occupation. Timor comes from the Malay "timur" meaning east.

Rock of Gibraltar – captured by the Umayyad commander Tariq ibn Ziyad in AD 711. The Rock's modern name derives from Jabal Tariq, or "Tariq's mountain" in Arabic.

Mississippi River – the largest river in the USA, its name means "big water", or "big river" in Algonquin.

Lake Nyasa – also known as Lake Malawi. Lying between Tanzania, Mozambique and Malawi, it is the third largest lake in Africa. "Nyasa" is a Swahili word for lake; the confusion can be blamed on the explorer David Livingstone who gave it the name in 1859.

Pendle Hill – the name of Pendle Hill in Lancashire is a triple tautology, combining words for "hill" in Cumbric, Old English and Modern English.

Sahara Desert – its name simply means "desert" in Arabic.

——— THE HAND OF GOD AND THE TEETH OF SUAREZ ———

A rogues' gallery of World Cup villains.

Chile and Italy, 1962 – the Battle of Santiago, as it came to be known. The levels of thuggery on the pitch required police involvement and inspired English referee Ken Aston to devise the red and yellow cards system. A stern-faced David Coleman introduced the BBC highlights: "The game you are about to see is the most stupid, appalling, disgusting and disgraceful exhibition of football in the history of the game."

West Germany and Austria, 1982 – in their final group game, West Germany and Austria contrived the 1–0 result that would send them both through at the expense of Algeria. The game was labelled the Disgrace of Gijón, or for the more historically-minded, the "Anschluss" game.

Harald Schumacher, 1982 – in a West German team packed with mullet-haired villains, goalkeeper Harald Schumacher excelled himself. In the semi-final match against a flamboyant France, he body-checked and knocked unconscious the defender Patrick Battiston who had been clean through on goal. The referee didn't even award a foul.

Diego Maradona, 1986 – England's bête noire. His outrageous handball in the quarter-final was followed four minutes later by a dribbled goal described by commentator Barry Davies as "pure football genius". The hand of God, however, was not his only indiscretion. He was sent off in his first World Cup in 1982, led an ill-disciplined Argentina team to the 1990 final and was expelled from the 1994 tournament for failing a drug test.

Frank Rijkaard, 1990 – the cultured Dutchman let himself down in the knock-out game against West Germany. He let loose a mouthful of spittle at German striker Rudi Völler after the pair had been sent off.

David Beckham, 1998 – before Goldenballs Beckham, there was Beckham the scapegoat, hanged in effigy outside a London pub. A sending-off for a sneaky kick at Diego Simeone in the round of 16 against Argentina ensured Beckham's status as a tabloid villain. His rehabilitation was exemplary and the boos soon faded.

Slaven Bilic, 1998 – the Croatian defender's face-clutching dive earned a red card for the popular French player Laurent Blanc in the World Cup semi-final. The first sending off of his career meant he missed the final of his home tournament.

Zinedine Zidane and Marco Materazzi, 2006 – the stage was set for the great Zinedine Zidane's final game, captaining France in the World Cup final in Berlin. At 1-1 in extra time he reacted to shirt-tugging and verbal provocation from the Italian defender Materazzi and floored him with a headbutt to the chest. He was red-carded (as he had been at the 1998 tournament) and his team went on to lose on penalties. His memorable last act as a footballer was immortalised in a sculpture by French artist Adel Abdessemed.

Luis Suarez, 2014 – in the 2010 World Cup quarter-final between Uruguay and Ghana, Suarez handled on the line to deny the Africans a winner in the last minute of extra-time. Four years later he was disgraced again after biting Italian defender Giorgio Chiellini. He had previous; it was the third time he'd nibbled on a fellow professional. The first incident while playing in Holland earned him the nickname the "Cannibal of Ajax".

—— THE WORLD'S OLDEST (BUT PROBABLY NOT FUNNIEST) JOKE ——

Dating to around 1900 BC, this comic aphorism had them chuckling in ancient Sumer (modern-day southern Iraq):

"Something which has never occurred since time immemorial; a young woman did not fart in her husband's lap."

The oldest recorded English joke suggests that 10th-century Anglo-Saxons would have felt at home with the *Carry On* films:

"What hangs at a man's thigh and wants to poke the hole that it's often poked before? A key."

--------------------- **DEAD AND UNBURIED** ---------------------

Bodies of the great and not so good preserved for posterity.

STILL ON DISPLAY

Vladimir Lenin – when the leader of the Russian Revolution died in 1924, his body was temporarily embalmed and displayed to the Soviet public. When the visiting crowds showed no sign of dwindling, the authorities decided to put it on view permanently. The "Lenin Lab" of scientists maintained the condition of his corpse, which was placed in a purpose-built mausoleum in Red Square. It has lain there ever since, apart from a brief exile to Siberia for safekeeping during the war and periodic removals for "maintenance".

Mao Zedong – the founding father of Communist China died suddenly in 1976. He had asked to be cremated but within a year of his death his body was on display in a memorial hall in Beijing's Tiananmen Square. Unusually, the embalming process was carried out without any assistance from Soviet scientists.

Ho Chi Minh – "Uncle Ho", the Vietnamese Communist leader (and former pastry cook in 1913 on the Newhaven-Dieppe ferry) can still be seen in his mausoleum in Hanoi.

Kim Il-Sung and Kim Jong-il – the father and son leaders of North Korea both now lie embalmed in the Kumsusan Palace of the Sun in Pyongyang. A former official residence, it is the largest such mausoleum in the Communist world. In death, its two inhabitants have been enshrined as "eternal leaders" of their country, according to a 2016 update to the North Korean constitution.

Jeremy Bentham – the preserved skeleton of Jeremy Bentham, English philosopher and founder of utilitarianism, sits in a glass cabinet at University College London. It is dressed in his own clothes and is topped with a wax head, the original having been taken away for safe keeping after it was stolen as a student prank. Bentham requested that he be displayed in this way in his will, written shortly before his death in 1832.

St Bernadette – the remains of Bernadette Soubirous are kept in a gold and crystal reliquary at a chapel in Nevers in France. Bernadette is celebrated in the Catholic Church for her visions of the Virgin Mary at Lourdes in 1858. She died in 1879 aged 35, but between 1909 and 1925 her body was exhumed three times and declared to be incorrupt. This "miraculous" discovery was offered as evidence of her sainthood and she was canonised in 1933. Visiting pilgrims today see wax coverings on her face and hands, depicting her appearance at the time of death.

NO LONGER ON SHOW

Joseph Stalin – after his death in 1953 his body was placed next to Lenin's in the Red Square mausoleum. Under Khrushchev's leadership the personality cult of Stalin was dismantled, and in 1961 he was quietly removed and buried by the Kremlin wall.

Khorloogiin Choibalsan – Stalinist dictator who ruled Mongolia for nearly two decades until 1952. The site of his former mausoleum is now a hall dedicated to that other Mongolian strongman, Genghis Khan.

Klement Gottwald – leader of the Czechoslovakian Communist Party. He died in 1953, shortly after attending Stalin's funeral. His preserved body was displayed in Prague until 1962.

Agostinho Neto – leader of the People's Republic of Angola, he died in Moscow in 1979 and was embalmed by the experts at the Lenin Lab. His body was on display in Luanda until 1990 when it was buried, in accordance with his widow's wishes.

Forbes Burnham – he dominated Guyana's post-independence politics first as prime minister and then president. He died in 1985, but his embalmed remains never actually went on display.

Georgi Dimitrov – the first Communist leader of Bulgaria, he died in 1949 and remained on public view until 1990. His mausoleum lasted another decade before it was destroyed after four attempts at demolition.

—————————— MOTHERS OF INVENTION ——————————

Inventions and innovations developed by women.

Computer programme – the daughter of the poet Lord Byron, Ada Lovelace was a mathematics prodigy. She collaborated with the polymath Charles Babbage, who had proposed a mechanical computer that he called the Analytical Engine. Lovelace published a step-by-step series of instructions detailing how Babbage's engine could be used to solve certain mathematical problems. This machine algorithm has been hailed as the first computer programme.

Dishwasher – Josephine Cochrane had grown tired of her best china getting chipped when the servants washed it. Doing the job herself was a tedious task, so she looked for a mechanical solution. The result was her hard-powered Dish Washing Machine, patented in 1886. It was a prize-winning design at the 1893 World's Columbian Exposition in Chicago and went into factory production four years later.

Windscreen wiper – in 1903, Mary Anderson from Alabama was awarded a patent for a "window-cleaning device" for cars.

Bobbinless sewing machine – one of the many inventions of Beulah Henry (1887–1973) of Memphis, nicknamed "Lady Edison". She was awarded a total of 49 patents, for devices ranging from a vacuum ice cream freezer to a child's doll whose eyes could change colour.

Torpedo radio guidance system – the Vienna-born actress Hedy Lamarr initially achieved notoriety for a brief nude appearance in the 1932 film *Ecstasy*. During the war, having fled to Hollywood, she co-designed a communications system for guiding torpedoes, using "frequency hopping" technology to prevent the signal being jammed. She was awarded a patent although the US Navy was slow to adopt the invention. It was, however, a precursor for today's GPS, wi-fi and Bluetooth technologies.

Kevlar – while working as a research chemist at DuPont in the 1960s, Stephanie Kwolek developed the nylon-like polymer that was trademarked as Kevlar. Five times stronger than steel (in terms of its strength-to-weight ratio) its applications include tyres, flame-resistant fabrics and bulletproof vests.

───── WHAT'S MY (REAL) NAME? ─────

Behind the stage names of rap and hip-hop.

50 Cent	Curtis Jackson
A$AP Rocky	Rakin Mayers
Afrika Bambaataa	Lance Taylor
Busta Rhymes	Trevor Smith
Cardi B	Belcalis Almanzar
Childish Gambino	Donald Glover
Coolio	Artis Ivey
Da Brat	Shawntae Harris
Diddy	Sean Combs
Dizzee Rascal	Dylan Mills
Drake	Aubrey Graham
Eminem	Marshall Mathers III
French Montana	Karim Kharbouch
Future	Nayvadius Wilburn
Ice Cube	O'Shea Jackson
Ice-T	Tracy Marrow
Jay-Z	Shawn Carter
Iggy Azalea	Amethyst Kelly
Lil Wayne	Dwayne Carter
Ludacris	Christopher Bridges
Lupe Fiasco	Wasalu Jaco
Nicki Minaj	Onika Maraj
Pitbull	Armando Pérez
Queen Latifah	Dana Owens
Rihanna	Robyn Fenty
Snoop Dogg	Cordozar Calvin Broadus
Stormzy	Michael Omari
The Game	Jayceon Taylor
The Notorious B.I.G.	Christopher Wallace
The Weeknd	Abel Tesfaye
Tinie Tempah	Patrick Okogwu
Vanilla Ice	Robert Van Winkle
Wiz Khalifa	Cameron Thomaz
Xzibit	Alvin Joiner

THE TRUTH IS OUT THERE

Some wacky conspiracy theories.

Jack the Ripper – the notorious killer who terrified Whitechapel in 1888 was none other than Prince Albert Victor, Duke of Clarence and Avondale, and the eldest son of the Prince of Wales. Or he was the acclaimed artist Walter Sickert, a theory that the crime writer Patricia Cornwell spent over £5 million trying to prove.

Alien landings and Area 51 – Area 51 exists; it's a secret installation in Nevada, administered by the Edwards Air Force Base. Officially it is known as the Nevada Test and Training Range at Groom Lake. UFOs have long been spotted in the area and it's claimed that the remains of crashed alien spacecraft are kept at the base. In 2017 it was confirmed that the Pentagon had indeed run an Advanced Aerospace Threat Identification Program. Keep watching the skies!

JFK assassination – the shooting that launched a thousand conspiracy theories. President Kennedy was shot in Dealey Plaza, Dallas in 1963 by Lee Harvey Oswald. Or perhaps by Oswald and another gunman standing on the grassy knoll. It was carried out on the orders of the American Mafia (or the CIA, the Cubans, the Russians or Vice President Lyndon B. Johnson).

Paul McCartney died in 1966 – he died in a car crash and was replaced by a look-alike. The theory goes that a visual clue was given on the cover of The Beatles' 1969 album *Abbey Road*. The number plate on the white VW Beetle car was LMW 28IF, indicating Paul would have been 28, if he'd lived.

Moon landings were faked – after the Russians sent the first man into space in 1961, the US staked its prestige on putting a man on the moon by the end of the decade. This was achieved by NASA's Apollo 11 mission in 1969. Or so it is widely believed. Others claim the moon landings were mocked up on a film set, perhaps even shot by the director Stanley Kubrick.

Elvis is alive – the King did not, in fact, die in 1977. He has been spotted at Memphis airport, Kalamazoo in Michigan and even sitting in the pool house back at Graceland. Perhaps Elvis never left the building after all.

AIDS was created by the CIA – in an attempt to decimate the gay and African-American populations, the CIA developed the AIDS virus in the 1970s.

9/11 was an inside job – the Twin Towers were destroyed by controlled explosions while the Pentagon was hit by a missile rather than a hijacked aircraft. A "false flag" operation, the September 11 attacks were used as a pretext by George W. Bush and Dick Cheney to launch America's wars for oil and dominance in the Middle East.

The world is controlled by lizards – the global elite who pull the strings in money and politics are actually the descendants of a race of extra-terrestrial shape-shifting reptiles. The man responsible for sharing this revelation is David Icke, the ex-Coventry goalkeeper and BBC sports presenter who identified himself as the son of God on Terry Wogan's chat show in 1991.

───────────────── **DEAD AT 27** ─────────────────

"I told him not to join that stupid club" – Kurt Cobain's mother.

Robert Johnson .... blues singer and guitarist, 1938
Rudy Lewis .... Drifters singer, 1964
Brian Jones .... founder of The Rolling Stones, 1969
Alan Wilson .... leader of Canned Heat, 1970
Jimi Hendrix .... electric guitarist and singer, 1970
Janis Joplin .... pioneering singer-songwriter, 1970
Jim Morrison .... lead singer of The Doors, 1971
Ron "Pigpen" McKernan .... member of the Grateful Dead, 1973
Pete Ham .... leader of Badfinger, 1975
Jean-Michel Basquiat .... New York artist, 1988
Kurt Cobain .... Nirvana frontman, 1994
Richey Edwards .... Manic Street Preachers member, disappeared 1995
Amy Winehouse .... singer-songwriter, 2011
Kim Jong-hyun .... Korean singer, 2017

——————— TRUMP INC. ———————

Donald Trump is worth an estimated $3.1 billion. These are businesses and products owned, sold, branded or endorsed by the reality TV star, Twitter troll and 45th President of the United States of America.

Property	The basis of his (partly inherited) fortune. Portfolio includes Trump Tower in New York.
Trump Hotels	Notably Chicago's Trump International Hotel & Tower, the fifth tallest building in the US.
Trump Entertainment Resorts	Casino and hospitality business that filed for Chapter 11 bankruptcy protection in 2004, 2009 and 2014.
Trump Golf	Courses including Turnberry in Scotland, four-time host of The Open Championship.
Trump Productions	TV production company, makers of *The Apprentice*.
Trump Shuttle	Defunct airline business.
GoTrump.com	Travel website launched in 2006. It promised "the art of the travel deal". It lasted barely a year.
Trump Steaks	The Donald's sales pitch was characteristically understated: "Believe me, I understand steaks. It's my favourite food. And these are the best!" It was discontinued in July 2007, two months after its introduction.
Trump Winery	Vineyards in the foothills of the Blue Ridge Mountains of Virginia.

Trump Natural Spring Water	"Proudly served at Trump Hotels, Restaurants and Golf Clubs worldwide".
Trump Vodka	Still available, in Israel.
Trump Mortgage	Casualty of the 2007 financial crisis.
Trump magazines	*Trump Style*, *Trump World* and *Trump Magazine*. No longer published.
Trump University	Offered courses, some costing up to $35,000, in property development, wealth creation and entrepreneurship. It ceased operations amid a flurry of lawsuits and in 2018 a court ordered $25m to be repaid to former students.
Trump: The Game	At the launch of the board game in 1989 Trump claimed it was "much more sophisticated than Monopoly, which I've played all my life". An *Apprentice*-inspired "I'm back and you're fired!" edition was released in 2004.
Trump apparel	Baseball caps, T-shirts, polo shirts, babywear and bibs.
Trump souvenirs	Including a Trump-branded gold bar piggy bank.
Donald Trump: The Fragrance	A 2004 partnership with Aramis that Trump claimed would be "the best men's scent available". He followed it up with fragrances called Success and Empire.

In the early 1990s the US satirical magazine *Spy* sent a series of cheques for tiny amounts to public figures. The magazine, which had infuriated Trump by dubbing him a "short-fingered vulgarian", revealed that the billionaire and self-proclaimed "very stable genius" had his price: $0.13 to be exact, judging by the cheque that he went to the trouble of cashing.

———— DON'T ASK FOR THESE AT THE LIBRARY ————

Books that only exist within other books.

Where God Went Wrong
Well, That About Wraps it Up for God
Some More of God's Greatest Mistakes
by Oolon Colluphid
(Douglas Adams, The Hitchhiker's Guide to the Galaxy series)

The Affair of the Second Goldfish
Death of a Debutante
The Cat It was who Died
The Death in the Drain Pipe
by Ariadne Oliver
(Agatha Christie, Hercule Poirot stories)

The History and Practice of English Magic
by Jonathan Strange
(Susanna Clarke, *Jonathan Strange & Mr Norrell*)

An Imperial Affliction
by Peter Van Houten
(John Green, *The Fault in Our Stars*)

Misery
Misery's Return
by Paul Sheldon
(Stephen King, *Misery*)

Necronomicon
by Abdul Alhazred
(H.P. Lovecraft, Cthulhu stories)

Camel Ride to the Tomb
Dogs Have No Uncles by X. Trapnel
Death's Head Swordsman: The Life and Works of X. Trapnel by
Russell Gwinnett

Fields of Amaranth by St John Clarke
Unburnt Boats by J.G. Quiggin
(Anthony Powell, A Dance to the Music of Time series)

The Theory and Practice of Oligarchical Collectivism
by Emmanuel Goldstein
(George Orwell, *Nineteen Eighty-Four*)

The Show Judges' Guide to Dragons
by Lady Sybil Ramkin
(Terry Pratchett, Discworld series)

The Heart is a Milkman
by Balph Eubank
(Ayn Rand, *Atlas Shrugged*)

A History of Magic
by Bathilda Bagshot
The Dark Forces: A Guide to Self-Protection
by Quentin Trimble
One Thousand Magical Herbs and Fungi
by Phyllida Spore
Home Life and Social Habits of British Muggles
by Wilhelm Wigworthy
(J.K. Rowling, Harry Potter series)

Ryder's Country Seats
Ryder's English Homes
by Charles Ryder
(Evelyn Waugh, *Brideshead Revisited*)

The Gutless Wonder
by Kilgore Trout
(Kurt Vonnegut, *Slaughterhouse Five*)

Travel Light
by Henry Bech
(John Updike, *Bech: A Book*)

—————— ISTANBUL, NOT CONSTANTINOPLE ——————

Cities that have changed their names since 1900.

In an old Russian joke a man was stopped and interrogated by the secret police: Where were you born? Saint Petersburg. Where did you go school? Petrograd. Where do you live? Leningrad. Where would you like to die? Saint Petersburg!

Bulgaria
Varna > Stalin > Varna

China
Peking > Beijing

*Democratic Republic of
the Congo*
Leopoldville > Kinshasa

Stanleyville > Kisangani

Germany
Chemnitz > Karl-Marx-Stadt >
Chemnitz

India
Bombay > Mumbai

Calcutta > Kolkata

Madras > Chennai

Indonesia
Batavia > Djakarta > Jakarta

Ireland
Kingstown >
Dún Laoghaire

Montenegro
Podgorica > Titograd >
Podgorica

Mozambique
Lourenço Marques > Maputo

Norway
Kristiania > Oslo

Russia
Saint Petersburg > Petrograd >
Leningrad > Saint Petersburg

Tsaritsyn > Stalingrad >
Volgograd

Königsberg > Kaliningrad

Nizhny Novgorod > Gorky >
Nizhny Novgorod

Yekaterinburg > Sverdlovsk >
Yekaterinburg

Tsarskoye Selo > Detskoye Selo
> Pushkin

Slovakia
Pressburg/Pozsony > Bratislava

Tajikistan
Dushanbe > Stalinabad >
Dushanbe

Sovietabad > Ghafurov

Turkey
Constantinople (Konstantiniyye)
> Istanbul

Smyrna > Izmir

Turkmenistan
Krasnovodsk > Turkmenbashi

Ukraine
Yuzovka > Trotsk > Stalino >
Donetsk

Lemberg > Lwów > Lviv

UK
Tunbridge Wells >
Royal Tunbridge Wells

Bognor > Bognor Regis

Wootton Bassett >
Royal Wootton Bassett

Vietnam
Saigon > Ho Chi Minh City

Zimbabwe
Salisbury > Harare

Many cities in the former Eastern Bloc were renamed to honour the heroes of Communism. Volgograd in Russia, Donetsk in Ukraine, Dushanbe in Tajikistan, Katowice in Poland, and Eisenhüttenstadt in Germany were all named after Joseph Stalin at various times.

–––––––––––– **GIVE 'EM ENOUGH ROPE** ––––––––––––

Capital punishment is on the wane across the world.

The last hanging took place in Britain in 1964. In France, the guillotine was used as recently as 1977. Now, Belarus is the only country in Europe that still uses the death penalty. In 2017, Amnesty International recorded at least 993 executions in 23 different countries. This figure excludes China, where an estimated 2,000 executions took place; the exact number is a closely-guarded state secret. Iran, Saudi Arabia, Iraq and Pakistan alone accounted for 84% of the total recorded by Amnesty. The USA is the only country in the Americas to use the death penalty, executing 23 people in 2017.

————————— **HAIL TO THE AUTHOR** —————————

Books by recent US presidents.

DONALD TRUMP
The Art of the Deal
Think Big and Kick Ass: In Business and in Life
Trump: Surviving at the Top
Trump: The Art of the Comeback
Why We Want You to Be Rich
Trump 101: The Way to Success
Time to Get Tough: Making America #1 Again
Crippled America: How to Make America Great Again

Trump's first book was published in 1987, the bestselling *The Art of the Deal*. During the 2016 presidential campaign his ghostwriter on that book, Tony Schwarz, gave him a less-than-ringing endorsement: "I genuinely believe that if Trump wins and gets the nuclear codes there is an excellent possibility it will lead to the end of civilization."

———————————————————————————————

BARACK OBAMA
Dreams from My Father: A Story of Race and Inheritance
The Audacity of Hope: Thoughts on Reclaiming the American Dream
Of Thee I Sing: A Letter to My Daughters

The Audacity of Hope became a US bestseller in 2006 after an endorsement from Oprah Winfrey, who described Obama as "her favourite senator".

———————————————————————————————

GEORGE W. BUSH
A Charge to Keep
Decision Points
41: A Portrait of My Father
*Portraits of Courage: A Commander in Chief's Tribute
   to America's Warriors*

After leaving office George W. Bush took up painting as a hobby. His *Portraits of Courage* is a collection of paintings of soldiers injured during the wars that marked his presidency. Its title echoes that of *Profiles in Courage*, the Pulitzer Prize-winning book by an earlier president, John F. Kennedy.

BILL CLINTON

Between Hope and History
My Life
Giving: How Each of Us Can Change the World
Back to Work: Why We Need Smart Government for a Strong Economy
The President is Missing (novel, written with James Patterson)

This is not the first work of fiction by a US president. That was the 2004 novel *The Hornet's Nest* by Jimmy Carter, a story set in the American South during the War of Independence.

GEORGE H.W. BUSH

All the Best: My Life in Letters and Other Writings
A World Transformed

RONALD REAGAN

An American Life

JIMMY CARTER

Keeping Faith: Memoirs of a President
Negotiation: The Alternative to Hostility
The Blood of Abraham: Insights into the Middle East
Talking Peace: A Vision for the Next Generation
The Little Baby Snoogle-Fleejer
The Virtues of Aging
An Hour before Daylight: Memories of a Rural Boyhood
We Can Have Peace in the Holy Land: A Plan That Will Work
A Full Life: Reflections at Ninety
(and 20 other works)

Still publishing books well into his tenth decade, Jimmy Carter is by far the most prolific writer of recent presidents.

———————— THE 21ST CENTURY IN QUOTES ————————

"You are the weakest link…goodbye."
**Anne Robinson, to departing contestants on the TV quiz
show *The Weakest Link*, 2000.**

"Are you ready? Okay. Let's roll."
**Todd Beamer, passenger on United Airlines Flight 93,
11 September 2001.**

"States like these and their terrorist allies constitute an axis of evil,
arming to threaten the peace of the world."
**President George W. Bush, referring to Iran, Iraq and North Korea
in his State of the Union address, 2002.**

"I am Saddam Hussein. I am the President of Iraq
and I am willing to negotiate."
**Saddam Hussein, after his capture by
US soldiers in December 2003.**

"Please don't call me arrogant, but I'm European champion
and I think I'm a special one."
**José Mourinho, at his first press conference as
manager of Chelsea FC, 2004.**

"The situation is untenable. It's just heartbreaking."
**Governor Kathleen Blanco of Louisiana on the devastation caused
by Hurricane Katrina, 2005.**

"I read the book. I read the script. I saw the movie
and I still don't understand it."
**Sean Connery, on why he opted not to play Gandalf in
The Lord of the Rings films, 2006.**

"Today Apple is going to reinvent the phone, and here it is."
Steve Jobs, introducing the iPhone, 2007.

"Yes we can!"
Barack Obama, campaign slogan, 2008.

"We're gonna be in the Hudson."
Chesley Sullenberger, US Airways Flight 1549 captain, 2009.

"She was just a sort of bigoted woman."
**Gordon Brown, caught on microphone describing Rochdale voter
Gillian Duffy, 2010.**

"I just killed a pig and a goat."
**Mark Zuckerberg, Facebook message after he'd vowed
to only eat animals he'd killed himself, 2011.**

"It's what I came here to do. I'm now a legend."
**Usain Bolt, after retaining his 100m and 200m titles
at the London Olympics, 2012.**

"I want every girl, every child, to be educated."
**Malala Yousafzai, Taliban shooting survivor
and education advocate, 2013.**

"I lost my balance, making my body unstable and falling on top
of my opponent. At that moment I hit my face against the player,
leaving a small bruise on my cheek and a strong pain in my teeth."
**Luis Suárez, explaining what caused him to bite Italian defender
Giorgio Chiellini at the World Cup, 2014.**

"I will build the greatest wall that you've ever seen."
Donald Trump, proposing a wall on the Mexican–US border, 2015.

"Take back control"
**Leave campaign slogan during the
UK's EU membership referendum, 2016.**

"There's a mistake. *Moonlight* – you guys won best picture."
**Jordan Horowitz, producer of *La La Land* after his film was
erroneously announced as Best Picture Oscar winner, 2017.**

"Do we kiss now?"
**Meghan Markle to her new husband, Prince Harry, as they posed on
the steps of St. George's Chapel, Windsor, 2018.**

—————— BORROWING FROM THE BARD ——————

George Bernard Shaw coined the term "bardolatry" for the excessive veneration of Shakespeare. Nevertheless, a host of different writers, artists and film-makers have borrowed titles for their works from lines in his plays.

HAMLET
North By Northwest – 1959 Alfred Hitchcock film, starring Cary Grant. From Hamlet's line: "I am but mad north-north-west".
Rosencrantz and Guildenstern are Dead – 1966 play by Tom Stoppard, inspired by the two minor characters who accompany Hamlet to England.
To Be Or Not To Be – 1942 satirical film, directed by Ernst Lubitsch (remade by Mel Brooks in 1983). In the film, a group of actors in Nazi-occupied Poland put on *Hamlet*, with the film's title coming from his famous soliloquy.
Infinite Jest – 1996 novel by David Foster Wallace. He took the title from Hamlet's description of Yorick in the gravedigging scene: "Alas, poor Yorick! I knew him, Horatio; a fellow of infinite jest…".

THE TEMPEST
Brave New World – 1932 dystopian novel by Aldous Huxley. The title comes from Miranda's exclamation "O brave new world, that has such people in't!"
Full Fathom Five – 1947 "drip" painting by Jackson Pollock. Named after a line "full fathom five thy father lies" in Ariel's song to Ferdinand.
Into Thin Air – 1997 factual account of a climbing disaster on Mount Everest by John Krakauer. The title is from part of Prospero's final speech to the audience: "Our revels now are ended. These our actors, as I foretold you, were all spirits, and are melted into air, into thin air…"

MACBETH
By the Pricking of My Thumbs – 1968 novel by Agatha Christie featuring the detectives Tommy and Tuppence Beresford. The title comes from the words the second witch uses to greet the return of Macbeth: "By the pricking of my thumbs, something wicked this way comes".

Something Wicked This Way Comes – 1962 fantasy novel by Ray Bradbury.

The Sound and the Fury – 1929 novel by William Faulkner. Named after Macbeth's weary assertion about life: "It is a tale told by an idiot, full of sound and fury, signifying nothing".

JULIUS CAESAR

The Dogs of War – 1974 Frederick Forsyth thriller about a band of mercenaries in Africa. Inspired by Mark Antony's vow to avenge the murdered Caesar: "Cry 'Havoc', and let slip the dogs of war".

The Fault in Our Stars – 2012 bestselling novel by John Green, adapted for the screen in 2014. The title is borrowed from Cassius's line: "The fault, dear Brutus, is not in our stars".

KING LEAR

Childe Roland to the Dark Tower Came – 1855 poem by Robert Browning. Its title comes from a fragment of nonsense verse spoken by Edgar while feigning madness.

OTHELLO

Pomp and Circumstance – series of marches composed by Edward Elgar. They are named after Othello's celebration of the "Pride, pomp and circumstance of glorious war!"

AS YOU LIKE IT

Under the Greenwood Tree – 1872 novel by Thomas Hardy, originally published anonymously. The title comes from the opening line of a song sung by Amiens.

TIMON OF ATHENS

Pale Fire – 1962 novel by Vladimir Nabokov. Timon describes the moon as "an arrant thief, and her pale fire she snatches from the sun".

TWELFTH NIGHT

Present Laughter – comic play by Noël Coward. The title is from a song by the fool Feste.

Cakes and Ale – novel by W. Somerset Maugham, inspired by Sir Toby Belch's complaint to Malvolio that "Dost thou think, because thou art virtuous, there shall be no more cakes and ale?"

—————— CALLING TIME ON DISEASE ——————

The May 1980 issue of the World Health Organization's official magazine declared on its front cover that "smallpox is dead". Vaccination programmes and improvements in public health worldwide are making some of history's greatest killers a thing of the past.

Smallpox – acute infectious disease that killed up to a third of its victims and left others permanently disfigured. In the late 18th century, English doctor Edward Jenner developed an effective vaccine against it. Smallpox is the first and so far the only major infectious disease in humans to be successfully eradicated through deliberate intervention. The World Health Organization began a global vaccination programme against smallpox in the 1960s and in 1980 declared the world free of the disease.

Rinderpest – viral disease in cattle, declared eradicated by the World Organisation for Animal Health in 2011. It is the first livestock disease to be eradicated by a vaccination programme.

Diseases targeted for elimination and eradication:

DISEASE	WORLDWIDE TOLL
Dracunculiasis (Guinea worm disease)	Only 30 reported cases in 2017 (down from over 800,000 in 1989).
Lymphatic filariasis (parasitic disease caused by thread-like worms)	36 million people estimated to suffer from chronic manifestations.
Measles	89,000 deaths in 2016 (below 100,000 for the first time).
Poliomyelitis (Polio)	22 recorded cases in 2017 (down 99% from 1988).
Rubella	Congenital rubella syndrome eliminated in many countries.

Taeniasis/cysticercosis (pork tapeworm)	Up to 50,000 deaths annually.
Leprosy	216,000 new cases reported in 2016.
Chagas disease (American trypanosomiasis)	6-7 million infected worldwide, mostly in Latin America.
Hepatitis B	Over 250 million people are living with a hepatitis B virus infection.
Iodine deficiency disorders	Not known, but being tackled by universal salt iodization.
Malaria	In 2016 there were an estimated 216 millon cases of malaria and 445,000 deaths.
Neonatal tetanus	Kills around 200,000 newborns each year, overwhelmingly in the developing world.
Onchocerciasis (river blindness)	18 million people infected, mainly in sub-Saharan Africa; 270,000 have suffered blindness.
Rabies	Around 50,000 deaths each year. 99% of cases involve infected dogs.
Trachoma	Around 2 million blind or visually impaired. 190 million at risk in trachoma endemic areas.
Yaws	Targeted for eradication in the 1950s, there are now only 13 countries where it is known to be endemic.

HAPPY ACCIDENTS

Serendipitous inventions.

Mauvine – the first successful synthetic dye was created accidentally in 1856 by student chemist William Perkin. He had been attempting to artificially produce the malaria cure quinine from coal tar when he stumbled upon the dye.

Petroleum jelly (Vaseline) – in 1859 the chemist Robert Chesebrough went to Titusville, Pennsylvania where oil had recently been discovered. He noticed that a naturally occurring by-product of the drilling process was being used by the riggers to treat cuts and burns.

X-rays – in 1895, Wilhelm Röntgen was putting an electric current through a cathode ray tube when he realised that a chemically-coated screen on a nearby bench was glowing. He began to study this mysterious radiation, which he called "x-rays". This discovery won him the very first Nobel Prize for Physics.

Safety (laminated) glass – in his laboratory in 1903, French scientist Edouard Benedictus knocked over a glass flask. It broke, but did not shatter, and he subsequently learned that it had been coated with cellulose nitrate.

Penicillin – the greatest accidental discovery of them all. Alexander Fleming later wrote: "When I woke up just after dawn on September 28, 1928, I certainly didn't plan to revolutionize all medicine by discovering the world's first antibiotic, or bacteria killer. But I guess that was exactly what I did." Returning to his London lab from a summer holiday he noticed that a culture of the bacteria staphylococcus was being attacked by a mould, penicillium notatum. Its clinical effectiveness was proved during the war and it has saved countless lives since.

Polytetrafluoroethylene (Teflon) – accidentally discovered in 1938 by chemist Roy Plunkett as a by-product of his research into new refrigerants.

Microwave oven – in 1945, while testing magnetrons (high-powered vacuum tubes inside radars) at the defence contractor Raytheon, engineer Percy Spencer saw that the chocolate bar in his pocket had melted. He began experimenting by placing various foods under the magnetron and within a couple of years the company had produced the first microwave oven.

Super glue – first discovered in 1942 by Harry Coover at Eastman Kodak while developing materials for plastic gun sights, but it was simply too sticky to be of practical use. It was re-discovered in 1951 when its commercial potential was understood. Originally marketed in 1958 as Eastman 910, it became known as super glue after it was successfully demonstrated on a TV panel show.

Post-it notes – the opposite story to super glue, these came about when a weak pressure-sensitive adhesive was created at the company 3M in 1968. It was over a decade before a commercial use for the glue was found.

---------------------- **KEEPING THE PEACE** ----------------------

There are currently 193 member states of the United Nations. The most recent countries to join were South Sudan in 2011, Montenegro in 2006 and Switzerland and East Timor, both in 2002. The Holy See and Palestine have permanent non-member observer status.

The United Nations Charter gives the Security Council the primary responsibility for maintaining international peace. It meets whenever this is threatened. It consists of 15 members: five permanent and ten non-permanent members. The non-permanent members are elected for a two-year term on a regional basis by the General Assembly.

Permanent members: China, France, Russia, UK and USA.

Non-permanent members: African and Asian states (5); Eastern European states (1); Latin American and Caribbean states (2); Western Europe and other states (2).

POWER MAD

Proof of Lord Acton's dictum that "Power tends to corrupt, and absolute power corrupts absolutely", here are some of the follies of those drunk with power.

Rafael Trujillo – President and dictator of the Dominican Republic from 1930 until his assassination in 1961. At the time of his death he was listed in *The Guinness Book of Records* as having more statues of himself in public places than any other world leader. The capital city and the nation's highest peak were renamed after him; his slogans appeared on car number plates and churches displayed the message "God in Heaven, Trujillo on Earth".

François "Papa Doc" Duvalier – President of Haiti from 1957–71. Papa Doc drew on traditional Haitian beliefs to create an aura of semi-divine invincibility. He announced in a speech that "bullets and machine guns capable of daunting Duvalier do not exist ... I am already an immaterial being". He claimed to have placed a voodoo curse on President Kennedy shortly before his assassination. Always fearful of the power of magic, Duvalier had all of Haiti's black dogs killed after being told an opponent could shapeshift into canine form.

Idi Amin – President of Uganda from 1971–9. Or to give him his full title, His Excellency President for Life, Field Marshal Al Hadji Doctor Idi Amin, VC, DSO, MC, CBE, Lord of all the Beasts of the Earth and Fishes of the Sea, and Conqueror of the British Empire in Africa in General and Uganda in Particular. He also claimed to be the uncrowned King of Scotland. His rule was characterised by brutality and ethnic strife, including the expulsion of the country's entire Asian population.

Jean-Bédel Bokassa – former French colonial soldier who became President of the Central African Republic in 1966 after seizing power in a coup. In 1976 he declared himself emperor of the newly created Central African Empire. In homage to his hero Napoleon he crowned himself in a lavish coronation ceremony that was estimated to have cost the same amount as his country's entire GDP. He was overthrown two years later amidst rumours of cannibalism.

Mobutu Sese Seko – President of Zaire (Democratic Republic of Congo) from 1965–97. He changed his country's name to Zaire in 1971, and the following year restyled himself from Joseph-Désiré Mobutu to Mobutu Sese Seko Koko Ngbendu Wa Za Banga (the all-powerful warrior who, because of his endurance and inflexible will to win, will go from conquest to conquest, leaving fire in his wake). For a brief period in 1975 the official media in Zaire was forbidden to mention any other person by name. An exemplary kleptocrat, Mobutu also proved to be an unlikely fashion innovator. He wore a distinctive leopard-skin toque hat and introduced the "abacost", an informal outfit whose name was a contraction of the French for "down with the suit". Mobutu had banned Western-style suits and ties in the name of his state policy of African "authenticity".

Kim Jong-il – North Korean premier from 1994–2011. And perhaps the world's greatest golfer, if the state media's story of his eleven holes-in-one in a single round is to be believed. An avid cinema fan, he organised the kidnapping in 1978 of one of South Korea's leading film directors and his actress ex-wife. They were forced to make films under Kim's tutelage until managing to escape the country in 1986. He died in 2011 and was succeeded by his youngest son Kim Jong-un, the third generation of the Kim dynasty to rule the country.

Saparmurat Niyazov – President of post-Soviet Turkmenistan from 1990–2006. From 1993 he styled himself Turkmenbashi ("father of the Turkmen") and set about creating the world's strangest personality cult. He banned opera and ballet, and outlawed long hair and beards for young men. All hospitals outside the capital Ashgabat were closed. The month of April was renamed after his mother. Numerous monuments were erected to himself, including a gold statue that rotated to face the rays of the Sun. His book *The Ruhnama*, a mixture of autobiography and spiritual musings, became a key part of the educational curriculum. Reading it three times a day, he assured an audience, was a short cut to heaven. And his advice for those with bad teeth? Don't get a gold crown, just gnaw on bones.

IN THEIR ELEMENT

Scientists honoured on the periodic table.

^{64}**Gd**
GADOLINIUM

Discovered in 1880 and named after the Finnish chemist Johan Gadolin who isolated yttria, the first rare earth metal to be identified.

^{96}**Cm**
CURIUM

Named for Pierre and Marie Curie, pioneering researchers into radioactivity. Marie Curie was the first woman to win a Nobel Prize (Physics, 1903) and the first person and only woman to win a second one (Chemistry, 1911, for the discovery of radium and polonium).

^{99}**Es**
EINSTEINIUM

No introduction needed. It honours the physicist who developed the general and special theories of relativity.

^{100}**Fm**
FERMIUM

Named for Enrico Fermi, the Italian physicist who created the world's first nuclear reactor in 1942, the Chicago Pile-1.

^{101}**Md**
MENDELEVIUM

Named for Dmitri Mendeleev, the Russian scientist who compiled the first accurate periodic table of elements.

^{102}**No**
NOBELIUM

Named for Alfred Nobel, the inventor of dynamite and founder of the Nobel Prizes.

^{103}**Lr**
LAWRENCIUM

Named for Ernest O. Lawrence, American scientist who was awarded the 1939 Nobel Prize for Physics for his invention of the cyclotron.

^{104}**Rf**
RUTHERFORDIUM

Named for the New Zealand-born physicist who discovered alpha and beta radiation, the atomic nucleus and named the proton.

--- **IN THEIR ELEMENT** ---

Scientists honoured on the periodic table.

106 Sg
SEABORGIUM
Named for US chemist Glenn T. Seaborg, known for his research into transuranic elements. First produced in the lab in 1974, Seaborgium was the first element named after a living person.

107 Bh
BOHRIUM
Named for Danish physicist Niels Bohr, winner of the Nobel Prize in 1922 for his work on the structure of atoms and radiation.

109 Mt
MEITNERIUM
Named for Lise Meitner, the Austrian-born physicist who helped formulate the theory of nuclear fission. It is the only element named solely for a female scientist.

111 Rg
ROENTGENIUM
Named for Wilhelm Röntgen, the discoverer of X-rays and the winner of the inaugural Nobel Prize in Physics in 1901.

112 Cn
COPERNICIUM
Named for Nicolas Copernicus, the Polish astronomer who proposed the heliocentric model of the solar system.

114 Fl
FLEROVIUM
Named for Russian physicist Georgy Flerov who founded the Joint Institute for Nuclear Research at Dubna, Russia, where the element was discovered in 1999.

118 Og
OGANESSON
Named for Russian nuclear physicist Yuri Oganessian, a former student of Flerov. It is, after seaborgium, only the second element named for a living person.

AN OFFER YOU CAN'T REFUSE

A whistle-stop tour of global organised crime.

USA
American Mafia – a shadow of the power it once was. The "five families" of New York have been rocked by informants and prosecutions, and Las Vegas is no longer a mob playground.

MS-13 – the Mara Salvatrucha emerged from the streets of Los Angeles; most of its members are of Central American origin. President Trump singled them out as a threat to law and order in 2017.

Mexican Mafia (La eMe) – despite its name, it did not originate in Mexico, but within the US prison system.

Crips and Bloods – African-American street gangs from Los Angeles. They're identified, respectively, by the blue and red colours worn by members.

Hells Angels – motorcycle gang that officially denies any involvement in illegal activities, although the US Department of Justice considers it a criminal organisation.

MEXICO
Drug cartels – Mexican groups such as Los Zetas, the Sinaloa, the Jalisco New Generation and the Gulf cartel control the lucrative drug routes into North America. In 2006, the Mexican government declared war on organised crime. The subsequent conflict between the authorities and the cartels has cost around 100,000 lives.

ITALY
Sicilian Mafia – emerged in the 19th century from bandit groups in rural Sicily. It is the original Mafia, or Cosa Nostra ("our thing") and spread to America through waves of emigration.

Camorra – organised crime group in and around Naples that inspired the TV series *Gomorrah*.

Ndrangheta – the Calabrian Mafia, whose name derives from a Greek word for heroism. They infamously kidnapped the grandson of the billionaire J. Paul Getty in 1973.

RUSSIA
Russian Mafia – Russian organised crime emerged in the Soviet era under the leadership of a criminal class known as "thieves in law". The collapse of the Soviet Union allowed the Russian Mafia to expand internationally.

CHINA
Triads – these criminal groups have their origins in secret societies formed in the 18th century. They are particularly entrenched in Hong Kong and in Chinese communities overseas.

Snakeheads – based in Fujian province, their core business is people smuggling.

JAPAN
Yakuza – the name comes from the Japanese for 8-9-3, a worthless hand of cards in a gambling game. Members are known for their distinctive body tattoos.

INDIA AND PAKISTAN
D-Company – the criminal group run by the fugitive gangster Dawood Ibrahim. He is wanted in India for his alleged involvement in a series of bombings in Mumbai in 1993.

JAMAICA
Yardies – violent criminal gangs who spread drug trafficking operations to the US and the UK. They originated in the poverty of the Kingston ghetto and the political violence that scarred Jamaica in the 1970s and '80s.

—————— READY PLAYER ONE ——————

From computer scientists playing around in the lab to eSports professionals battling it out in packed stadiums, video games have come a long way. These are some of the games that broke the mould.

Spacewar! – invented in 1962 by a student at MIT, it was the first computer-based video game. It consisted of a duel between two spaceships rotating around a star.

Pong – not actually the first arcade game (Computer Space got there first) but the 1972 tennis game Pong was a US hit and helped establish the video games industry. The first home video games console, the Magnavox Odyssey, debuted in the same year.

Space Invaders – developed by Tomohiro Nishikado and launched in Japan in 1978. The video games business had gone global.

Pac-Man – partly inspired by a pizza that was missing a slice, Pac-Man became an icon of popular culture in the 1980s, inspiring a children's cartoon and countless items of merchandise. It was recognised by Guinness World Records as the world's most successful coin-operated arcade game.

Elite – trading game, set in space, written for the BBC Micro and Acorn Electron home computers in 1984. The 3-D graphics and the open-ended gameplay were innovations.

Tetris – the bestselling video game of all time with around half a billion sales. Invented in 1984 by the Soviet computer engineer Alexey Pajitnov and inspired by the shape puzzles of his childhood.

Super Mario Bros – Mario first appeared as "Jumpman" in the arcade game Donkey Kong. Now, alongside his brother Luigi, he starred in a bestselling series that helped make Nintendo the pre-eminent gaming company. A 1993 film starred Bob Hoskins as Mario.

Doom – first-person shooter games were not new, but Doom cemented the genre and pioneered networked multiplayer gaming. It spawned a series of sequels.

FIFA – football video game, launched in 1993 by EA Sports. A new version has been issued every year since and it is the world's best-selling sports game series.

Tomb Raider – the aristocratic archaeologist Lara Croft became a video game icon, acclaimed by many as a strong female protagonist and decried by others as over-sexualised. She was portrayed on screen first by Angelina Jolie and then Alicia Vikander in a 2018 film reboot.

The Sims – launched in 2000, it was a life simulation that lacked the structure and strictly-defined goals of more traditional games. Intended as a satire of consumer culture, it was the breakthrough example of the "sandbox" genre.

Grand Theft Auto III – players roamed Liberty City, leaving mayhem in their wake. Its violence and sexual content attracted criticism but the open world design was revolutionary.

World of Warcraft – the most popular massively multiplayer online role-playing game (MMORPG) ever. So far, over 100 million accounts have been created to play the game.

Angry Birds – it made the mobile phone credible as a gaming platform and established the business model of a free game augmented by paid-for micro-transactions.

League of Legends – the most popular game in eSports, an industry with a projected revenue in 2018 of almost a billion dollars. The LoL world championships grand final in 2017 had a peak audience of 28 million online viewers.

Pokémon Go – players took to the streets searching for digital creatures in the real world. The augmented reality game was launched in 2016 and by the end of the year the app had been downloaded 500 million times.

Fortnite: Battle Royale – up to 100 players fight for survival on an island. Since its release in 2017 it has attracted over 125 million devotees, inspired dance crazes and been blamed for classroom disruption.

NOT QUITE DEADLIER THAN THE MALE

Female would-be assassins who didn't quite hit the mark.

Khioniya Guseva – a noseless woman who stabbed the Russian mystic and "mad monk" Grigori Rasputin in 1914, while he was on a visit back to his home village of Pokrovskoye in western Siberia. After plunging a knife into his abdomen she cried "I have killed the Antichrist!" She hadn't, and he lived for another two years before being murdered by a group led by Prince Felix Yusupov.

Fanny Kaplan – member of the Socialist Revolutionary Party who shot Russian leader Vladimir Lenin on 30 August 1918 as he left the Hammer and Sickle factory in Moscow. Arrested at the scene she declared him to be a "traitor to the revolution". Lenin survived the attempt, and soon introduced the savage political repression known as the Red Terror.

Violet Gibson – the daughter of a former Lord Chancellor of Ireland, in 1926 she shot at Benito Mussolini on the steps of the Capitol in Rome. He escaped with a grazed nose, while she was later deported to England and detained in an asylum.

Ruth Steinhagen – in 1949 she shot the Philadelphia Phillies baseball player Eddie Waitkus in a Chicago hotel room. It is regarded as one of the first recorded cases of stalking and inspired the Robert Redford film *The Natural*.

Valerie Solanas – radical feminist and author of the Manifesto for SCUM (Society for Cutting Up Men), she shot and critically wounded the artist Andy Warhol in 1968. She was angry that Warhol had apparently lost the copy that she'd given him of her play *Up Your Ass*. Unrepentant, she said afterwards "I should have done target practice."

Lynette "Squeaky" Fromme – member of the notorious "Manson family", she tried to assassinate US President Gerald Ford in Sacramento in 1975. Her alleged motive was concern over the effect of pollution on California's giant redwood trees. She brandished a pistol, but failed to fire a shot. She remained in prison until her release on parole in 2009.

Sara Jane Moore – 17 days after Fromme's attempt, Moore shot at Ford in San Francisco. She spent 32 years in prison, before being released in 2007.

GOING UNDERGROUND

The world's subway systems in superlatives.

Oldest – London. In 1863, the Metropolitan Railway opened the world's first underground railway between Paddington (then Bishop's Road) and Farringdon Street.

Busiest – Tokyo. Passengers in the world's largest metropolis collectively make over 3 billion metro journeys a year.

Most stations – New York. It has 472 stations serving 27 subway lines, more than any other system.

Longest – Shanghai. Only opened in 1993, the Shanghai Metro is the longest rapid transit system in the world with 644km of route length.

Deepest – Arsenalna station in Kiev is the deepest single station at 105m. St Petersburg in Russia and Pyongyang in North Korea both claim to be the deepest on average.

FOOTBALL'S GONE MAD (AGAIN)

The progression of professional football's world transfer fee record.

Year	Player	Selling club	Buying club	Fee (£)
1893	Willie Groves	WBA	Aston Villa	100
1905	Alf Common	Sunderland	Middlesbrough	1,000
1928	David Jack	Bolton	Arsenal	10,890
1961	Luis Suárez	Barcelona	Internazionale	152,000
1975	Giuseppe Savoldi	Bologna	Napoli	1,200,000
1992	Jean-Pierre Papin	Marseille	AC Milan	10,000,000
2017	Neymar	Barcelona	PSG	198,000,000

---------------- **STRANGEST WARS EVER FOUGHT** ----------------

We all know it's good for nothing. People and sometimes emus get hurt.

War of the Bucket – (1325) Fought between the Italian city-states of Modena and Bologna. The war was sparked off by the theft of a bucket from a well in Bologna by a group of Modenese soldiers. It is still proudly displayed at Modena's Palazzo Comunale as a reminder of the city's victory in the subsequent Battle of Zappolino.

War of the Two Pedros – (1356–69) Protracted border fighting between Pedro "the Cruel" of Castile and Pedro IV of Aragon.

War of the Three Henrys – (1587–89) Part of the French Wars of Religion. The three Henrys were King Henry III, Henry of Bourbon (later Henry IV) and Henry of Lorraine.

War of Jenkins' Ear – (1739–48) Conflict between Britain and Spain over commercial and imperial rivalries. Named after Captain Robert Jenkins whose ear was alleged to have been cut off by Spanish coast guards in the West Indies.

War of the Oranges – (1801) Brief Spanish invasion of Portugal.

Pig War – (1859) Border dispute between the US and British over the San Juan Islands in modern-day Washington state. The only casualty was an unruly pig that strayed into an American farmer's potato patch.

War of the Golden Stool – (1900) Conflict in Ghana between the Ashanti Empire and British imperial authorities. The Gold Coast governor Sir Frederick Hodgson provoked furious opposition by demanding he be given the Golden Stool, the symbol of Ashanti sovereignty.

War of the Stray Dog – (1925) Dispute between Greece and Bulgaria. A Greek soldier attempting to retrieve his dog was shot by a Bulgarian sentry, prompting a border skirmish that was eventually defused by the League of Nations. The fate of the dog is unknown.

Great Emu War – (1932) An attempt by the army to cull emus in the Campion district of Western Australia. It failed. The artillery commander Major G.P.W. Meredith ruefully said later: "If we had a military division with the bullet-carrying capacity of these birds, it would face any army in the world."

Football War – (1969) El Salvador and Honduras. Rioting at qualifying matches for the 1970 World Cup lit the fuse for a brief conflict between these Central American neighbours.

Cod Wars – (1958–61 and 1972–3) Disputes between Britain and Iceland over fishing rights in the North Atlantic.

MINING FOR MOBILES

An iPhone will typically contain around 25g of aluminium, 15g of copper, approximately 0.034g of gold, 0.34g of silver, 0.015g of palladium and less than one-thousandth of a gram of platinum. These are the metals in your mobile.

Aluminium – used for phone casings and other components.
Cobalt – used in lithium-ion rechargeable batteries.
Copper – in the circuit board as a conductor of electricity.
Gold – small amounts are used in the circuit board.
Indium – LCD displays.
Lead – used in the solder that keeps the phone components together.
Lithium – in mobile phone batteries.
Nickel – in electrical connections, batteries and capacitors.
Platinum group metals – capacitors, circuitry and plating.
Potassium – strengthens glass in the touchscreen.
Silver – the best conductor of electricity, it's used on circuit boards.
Tantalum – rare metal, used in capacitors.
Tin – used in LCD displays and circuit board solder.
Tungsten – highly durable and dense, it's used in the phone vibration system.
Zinc – also used in the circuit board.

———— LECHEROUS AS A MONKEY … OR A SPARROW? ————

Common, and uncommon, animal similes.

Angry as a hornet
Bald as a coot
Big as a whale
Blind as a bat
Brave as a lion
Busy as a bee
Cheeky as a monkey
Cold as a fish
Dead as a dodo
Drunk as a skunk
Fat as a pig
Free as a bird
Graceful as a swan
Gentle as a lamb
Happy as a lark
Hungry as a horse
Lecherous as a monkey
   (from *Henry IV Part 2*)
Lecherous as a sparrow
   (from *The Canterbury Tales*)
Loathsome as a toad
   (from *Titus Andronicus*)

Mad as a March hare
Nervous as a cat
Pert as a magpie
Poor as a church mouse
Quiet as a mouse
Proud as a peacock
Rank as a fox
   (from *Twelfth Night*)
Sick as a dog
Silly as a goose
Slippery as an eel
Sly as a fox
Snug as a bug in a rug
Strong as an ox
Stubborn as a mule
Sweet as a nightingale's song
Swift as a swallow
Tall as a giraffe
Ugly as a bear (from *A
   Midsummer Night's Dream*)
Weak as a kitten
Wet as a drowned rat

———————— CHANGING SONGS IN MID-STREAM ————————

Founded in 2006, the Swedish service Spotify is the world leader in online music streaming. These are its all-time most streamed songs (as of August, 2018).

Rank	Song	Artist	Streams (m)
1	Shape of You	Ed Sheeran	1,867
2	One Dance	Drake ft. Wizkid and Kyla	1,534
3	Closer	The Chainsmokers	1,341
4	rockstar	Post Malone ft. 21 Savage	1,182

JOINING THE PARTY

The membership of the European Union. The UK won't actually be the first territory to leave; Greenland formally withdrew in 1985 following its own referendum.

1957 – original members: Belgium, France, Germany, Italy, Luxembourg and the Netherlands.
1973 – first expansion: UK, Ireland and Denmark join.
1981 – Greece enters.
1986 – Spain and Portugal join.
1995 – fourth enlargement: Austria, Finland and Sweden.
2004 – fifth, and biggest, expansion: Czech Republic, Estonia, Cyprus, Latvia, Lithuania, Hungary, Malta, Poland, Slovakia and Slovenia.
2007 – Romania and Bulgaria become members.
2013 – Croatia becomes the 28th country to join the EU.
2019 – following the 2016 referendum, the UK is scheduled to leave the EU on 29 March 2019.

SCENT OF A CELEBRITY

The launch of Elizabeth Taylor's Passion fragrance in 1987 marked the beginning of a new, and highly profitable, era in the perfume business. Now, few of the biggest stars are without their own scent endorsement.

Beyoncé – Heat, Pulse, Rise
Justin Bieber – Someday, Girlfriend, Next Girlfriend
Cheryl (Tweedy, Cole, Fernandez-Versini) – Storm Flower
Lady Gaga – Fame, Eau de Gaga
Sean John (aka Diddy) – Unforgiveable, 3 AM, I am King
Jennifer Lopez – Glow, JLove, JLust
One Direction – You & I, Between Us, Our Moment
Sarah Jessica Parker – Covet, Stash, Lovely
Katy Perry – Killer Queen, Royal Revolution, Meow
Rihanna – Nude, Rogue, Reb'l Fleur
Britney Spears – Curious, Fantasy, Believe
Kim Kardashian West – Fleur Fatale, Body, Crystal Gardenia
Taylor Swift – Incredible Things, Taylor, Wonderstruck

——————— DRESSED TO THRILL ———————

Fashion statements that raised eyebrows and hackles.

Marilyn Monroe's white dress in the 1955 film *The Seven Year Itch*. Monroe standing on a New York subway grating as a rush of air blows her dress upwards is one of cinema's enduring images. Once owned by the actress Debbie Reynolds as part of her Hollywood memorabilia collection, the dress from *The Seven Year Itch* was sold at auction in 2011 for $4.6m.

Audrey Hepburn's sleeveless evening gown in *Breakfast at Tiffany's*. The Givenchy-designed little black dress helped cement Hepburn's status as an icon of elegance.

Jackie Kennedy's pink Chanel suit. This outfit is indelibly and tragically linked to the images of 22 November 1963. She wore it, stained with her husband's blood, as Lyndon B. Johnson was sworn in as president on Air Force One.

Liz Hurley's safety-pin dress, worn to the 1994 premiere of *Four Weddings and a Funeral*. The Versace design created a media sensation and ensured that Hurley eclipsed then-boyfriend and star of the film, Hugh Grant.

Geri Halliwell's Union Jack dress at the 1997 Brit Awards. It was originally a plain Gucci black mini-dress but Geri's sister spiced it up by sewing on a Union Jack tea towel.

Björk's white swan dress was designed by Marjan Pejoski and was worn several times including on the red carpet at the Academy Awards in 2001. Much mocked and parodied at the time, it was displayed at New York's Museum of Modern Art in 2015.

Lady Gaga's meat dress at the 2010 MTV Video Music Awards. Designed by Franc Fernandez and made of raw beef, it appalled and fascinated in equal measure.

Kate Middleton's wedding dress in 2011, designed by Sarah Burton for Alexander McQueen. Within days of her marriage to Prince William, replicas of the dress were on sale across the world.

—————————— **WE'RE ALL X-MEN** ——————————

Genetic mutations that many of us share.

Blue eyes – originally, all humans had brown eyes. The emergence of blue eyes is thanks to a genetic change that took place less than 10,000 years ago. So, Frank Sinatra was a mutant? In his way, yes.

Red hair – it is rare in humans, though most common in people of northern European ancestry. It's caused by the inactivity of a gene that governs eumelanin, the pigment that gives hair a dark colour.

Drinking milk – lactose intolerance isn't a genetic mutation. Actually, the reverse is true. The ability of adults to digest milk is thanks to a mutation of the MCM6 gene that occurred around 10,000 years ago when humans first domesticated dairy animals.

Red face after drinking – the alcohol flush reaction affects around a third of the population of East Asia.

Missing wisdom teeth – human fossils from China dating from over 300,000 years ago have been found without wisdom teeth.

Colour blindness – it chiefly affects men because the genes for red and green cone cells on the retina are on the X chromosome.

—————————— **DECOMPOSING COMPOSERS** ——————————

It's not just their music that was baroque, but their deaths, too.

Jean-Baptiste Lully – Italian-born composer who died of gangrene in 1687 after injuring his foot with a stick while beating time during a performance.

Michael Wise – Salisbury organist and composer who was killed in 1687 after picking a fight with a night watchman following a furious row with his wife.

Frantisek Kotzwara – Czech musician and composer who died in London in 1791 in one of the first recorded cases of erotic asphyxiation.

IF SOMETHING CAN GO WRONG...

Rules of thumb for life, work and online discourse.

Betteridge's law of headlines
Any newspaper headline that ends in a question mark can be answered by the word "no".

Arthur C. Clarke's third law
Any sufficiently advanced technology is indistinguishable from magic.

Cunningham's law
The best way to get the right answer online is not to ask a question, it's to post the wrong answer.

Godwin's law
As an online discussion grows longer, the probability of a comparison involving the Nazis or Hitler approaches 1.

Murphy's (or Sod's) law
Anything that can go wrong will go wrong.

Occam's razor
Multiplicity ought not to be posited without necessity. Or to put it simply, when various hypotheses exist, the one requiring the fewest assumptions should be preferred.

Pareto's law
80% of the effects are achieved by 20% of the causes.

Peter principle
Workers tend to be promoted to the level just above their competence, thereby creating incompetent senior management in any organisation.

Sutton's law
In medical diagnosis, consider the obvious explanation first. It takes its name from the (probably apocryphal) reply from the criminal Willie Sutton when asked why he robbed banks: "because that's where the money is".

Parkinson's law
Work expands to fill the time available for its completion.

Parkinson's law of triviality
The time spent on any item of an agenda will be in inverse proportion to the sum involved.

Sagan standard
Extraordinary claims require extraordinary evidence.

NATURE'S BIGGEST GATHERINGS

Some species can occupy the equivalent of an entire country when word gets out that there's a get-together.

Starlings – giant flocks of starlings, known as "murmurations", typically contain around 100,000 birds. But they can grow much larger; in the winter of 1999–2000 a murmuration of an estimated 6 million starlings was observed at Shapwick Heath reserve on the Somerset Levels, UK.

Red-billed quelea – thought to be the most populous wild bird species in the world. Native to Africa, they form colonies of up to 30 million birds. Their feeding can have a devastating effect on crops, earning them the nickname of the "feathered locust".

Herring – schools of North Atlantic herring can extend across six square miles and contain over a billion fish.

Ants – a "super colony" of billions of Argentine ants was identified in 2002 stretching 3,700 miles from Spain, across southern France, to northern Italy.

Locusts – a swarm of Rocky Mountain locusts reported in the USA in 1875 may be the greatest-ever gathering of any living creature. Covering an area 1,800 miles long and 110 miles wide, the swarm was estimated to have contained 12 trillion locusts (weighing some 27 million tons). Astonishingly, despite these vast numbers, the Rocky Mountain locust was extinct within 30 years.

THE GREAT FIREWALL OF CHINA

China's Internet is one of the most rigidly controlled in the world; the state employs more than two million people to monitor online activity. This is just a sample of terms that have been censored on the popular microblogging site Weibo.

Winnie the Pooh (and Disney)
Images of the honey-loving bear have been widely used to mock Chinese President Xi Jinping.

1984 and Animal Farm
George Orwell's treatments of dictatorship.

Brave New World
Aldous Huxley's dystopian novel.

My emperor
In February 2018, the National People's Congress approved constitutional changes removing the two-term limit on Chinese presidents. This opens the possibility of Xi remaining in power for life.

The Emperor's Dream
1947 animated film.

Long live

Change the law

Ascend the throne

Roll up sleeves – phrase used in Xi's 2017 New Year message.

Wheel of history

I'm willing to be a vegetarian for the rest of my life
Allusion to a TV historical drama in which an empress makes this Buddhist vow in return for the death of the emperor.

Disagree

Emigrate

Incapable ruler

Personality cult

Letter 'N'

For only a matter of hours after the Chinese Communist Party released the proposal to scrap presidential term limits; the reason still remains unclear.

EXIT VIA THE KUIPER BELT

The Kuiper belt is an area of the outer solar system, beyond the orbit of Neptune, stretching across 20 astronomical units (AU) – around 1.86 billion miles. It contains numerous icy objects including comets and minor planets. Some man-made objects have made it this far, including:

Voyager 1 – the most distant man-made object. Launched by NASA in 1977, it flew past Jupiter in 1979 and Saturn in 1980. It entered interstellar space in 2012 and is now thought to be 141 AU (around 13 billion miles) away. In 40,000 years it will pass by the star Gilese 445, located 17.6 light years from Earth.

Pioneer 10 – launched in 1972, it was the first probe to reach Jupiter. Around 120 AU (over 11 billion miles) from Earth.

Voyager 2 – launched in 1977, it had close encounters with Jupiter, Saturn, Uranus and Neptune. Currently it's 116 AU from home.

Pioneer 11 – launched in 1973, it is 99 AU from Earth, heading towards the centre of the Milky Way. In around 4 million years it will pass near the star Lambda Aquila.

New Horizons – launched in 2006, it flew past Pluto in 2015 and will soon study other objects in the Kuiper belt at a distance of around 40 AU.

SHORT, FAT AND BALD

Some less-than-flattering royal bynames.

The Apostate – Julian, Roman emperor from AD 361–3. An opponent of Christianity, he restored paganism as the state religion.

The Dung-named – Constantine V, Byzantine emperor from 741–75.

The Short – Pepin III, king of the Franks from 754–68. The father of Charlemagne.

The Hunchback – Pepin, eldest son of Charlemagne, died 811.

The Bald – Charles II, king of France from 843–77.

The Stammerer – Louis, king of France, 877–9.

The Simple – Charles III, king of France from 893–922.

The Do-Nothing – Louis V, king of France, 986–7.

The Boneless – Ivar, Viking leader, died c. 870.

Bluetooth – Harald, king of Denmark, c. 958–c. 985. The wireless communications technology is named after him.

The Unready – Ethelred II, king of England from 978–1016. His nickname is derived from "unraed" (badly-advised) and is a pun on Ethelred, which means "noble counsel".

The Bastard – William, Duke of Normandy and king of England from 1066–87. He'd probably prefer to be remembered as William the Conqueror.

The Fat – Louis VI, king of France from 1108–37.

The Cabbage – Ivaylo, tsar of Bulgaria, 1278–9.

Lackland (or Softsword) – John, king of England, 1199–1216. The names refer, respectively, to his meagre inheritance and failure in war. The chronicler Matthew Paris wrote: "foul as it is, Hell itself is defiled by the fouler presence of John".

The Lisping and Lame – Erik Eriksson, king of Sweden in 1222–9 and 1234–50.

Toom Tabard (Empty Cloak) – John Balliol, king of Scots, 1292–6.

The Mad – Charles VI, king of France, 1380–1422. Grandfather of Henry VI of England, who seemingly inherited his mental incapacity.

The Impotent – Henry IV of Castile from 1454–74.

Universal Spider – Louis XI, king of France 1461–83.

Crookback – Richard III, king of England 1483–5 and resident of a Leicester car park until 2012. His nickname wasn't merely Tudor propaganda, however. When it was dug up his skeleton showed evidence of scoliosis (curvature of the spine).

The Mad – Joanna, queen of Castile and León from 1504–55. Mother of the mighty Emperor Charles V.

The Silent – William, Prince of Orange, from 1544–84. The first head of state to be assassinated with a handgun.

Wisest Fool in Christendom – James I and VI, king of England 1603–25 (after the union of the English and Scottish crowns) and king of Scotland from 1567.

GOING ROUND IN CIRCLES 3

The countries you pass through while travelling along some of the Earth's imaginary lines.

The Equator (East from the prime meridian)
São Tomé and Principe • Gabon • Republic of the Congo • DR Congo • Uganda • Kenya • Somalia • Indonesia • Ecuador • Colombia • Brazil

———————— LARGE HADRON COLLIDER: ————————
SCIENCE AT (JUST UNDER) THE SPEED OF LIGHT

The Large Hadron Collider (LHC) is the most powerful particle accelerator ever built. So where does the name come from?

Large – almost 27km in circumference and located 100m underground at CERN (European Organization for Nuclear Research) on the Franco-Swiss border near Geneva.

Hadron – it accelerates protons and ions, which are particles classed as baryons, which belong to the hadron family of particles.

Collider – beams made up of particles travel in opposite directions, colliding at four points.

How does it work?
The accelerator complex at CERN is a chain of machines with increasingly higher energies. As a beam of particles is passed from one to another it successively gains more energy. The LHC is the final element of this series, where the beams reach their highest energy levels. Before they collide inside the LHC, the two particle beams are travelling at close to the speed of light. The superconducting electromagnets that guide them are chilled to a temperature of -271.3°C or 1.9K (kelvins). That's colder than the -270.5°C of outer space. The LHC produces up to 1 billion proton collisions per second.

What is it looking for?
It's seeking answers to questions that are not fully explained by the Standard Model of particle physics. For example: what are dark energy and dark matter? Why does there appear to be more matter than anti-matter in the universe? What is the origin of mass? A key piece in this puzzle was the discovery at the Large Hadron Collider in 2012 of the Higgs bosun. This particle had been proposed in the 1960s but had not been verified by experimental investigation. François Englert and Peter Higgs duly won the Nobel Prize in Physics in 2013 "for the theoretical discovery of a mechanism that contributes to our understanding of the origin of mass of subatomic particles, and which recently was confirmed through the discovery of the predicted fundamental particle, by the ATLAS and CMS experiments at CERN's Large Hadron Collider".

———————— STRESSED OUT? ————————

In the 1960s, the psychiatrists Thomas Holmes and Richard Rahe devised a Social Readjustment Rating Scale that ranked the stress levels caused by 43 different life events. This is the top 20. A combined total of 150+ in a 12-month period is a cause for concern.

Death of a spouse 100
Divorce 73
Marital separation 65
Imprisonment 63
Death of close family member 63
Personal injury or illness 53
Marriage 50
Dismissal from work 47
Marital reconciliation 45
Retirement 45
Change in health of family member 44
Pregnancy 40
Sexual difficulties 39
Gain a new family member 39
Business readjustment 39
Change in financial state 38
Death of a close friend 37
Change to a different line of work 36
Change in frequency of arguments 35
Large mortgage 32

"One of the symptoms of an approaching nervous breakdown is the belief that one's work is terribly important."

Bertrand Russell, English philosopher, 1930.

─────────── **IT'S GETTING HOT IN HERE** ───────────

Some inconvenient truths from the United Nations Intergovernmental Panel on Climate Change.

1. Human influence on the climate system is clear. Recent anthropogenic (human-made) emissions of greenhouse gases are the highest in history. And recent climate changes have had a widespread impact on human and natural systems across the world.

2. Warming of the climate system is unequivocal. Since the 1950s many of the observed changes are unprecedented over the short and long term, from decades to thousands of years. The atmosphere and oceans have warmed; the amounts of snow and ice have fallen; and sea levels have risen.

3. Man-made greenhouse gas emissions have increased since the pre-industrial era, driven by population and economic growth, and are now higher than ever. This has led to atmospheric concentrations of carbon dioxide, methane and nitrous oxide that are unprecedented in at least the last 800,000 years. This is likely to be the major cause of the global warming observed since the mid-20th century.

4. Changes in the pattern of extreme weather and climate events have been observed since about 1950. Some of these changes have been linked to human activity, including a decrease in cold temperature extremes and an increase in hot temperature extremes. Greenhouse gas emissions are also blamed for an increase in extreme sea levels and the number of heavy rainfall incidences.

5. Continued emission of greenhouse gases will cause further warming and long-lasting changes in the global climate. Surface temperatures are predicted to rise during the 21st century in every envisaged emission scenario. Heatwaves will be become more frequent and more severe; extreme rainfall will become more frequent; oceans will become warmer and more acidic; sea levels will rise.

——————————— **UP IN SMOKE** ———————————

On the vapour trail of e-cigarettes.

Although the first patent for a "smokeless non-tobacco cigarette" was filed in 1963, the modern e-cigarette is the invention of the Beijing pharmacist Hon Lik who introduced it to the Chinese domestic market in 2004.

E-cigarettes, sometimes known as ENDS (electronic nicotine delivery systems) consist of a battery, a heating element and a reservoir of liquid. It produces the vapour cloud by heating a liquid containing nicotine, flavourings and other chemicals. This is inhaled by users (and any passers-by who happen to be standing too close). While generally considered to be better for you than smoking tobacco, there are health concerns over vaping. Nicotine, of course, is highly addictive and harmful to developing foetuses and adolescent brains. The e-cigarette aerosol also contains carcinogenic chemicals and ultrafine particles that can damage the lungs. And, once in a while, they explode. In May 2018, a post-mortem confirmed that a Florida man had died when a vape pen blew up and projected fragments into his skull.

In Britain around 6% of adults vape, with most using it as an aid to stopping smoking. The most popular flavours are fruit (29%), tobacco (27%) and menthol or mint (25%).

——————————— **IS THAT YOUR FINAL ANSWER?** ———————————

Five people have won the top prize on the UK quiz show *Who Wants to be a Millionaire?* These are the answers to their final questions on page 47.

1. b
2. a
3. c
4. a
5. a

COINING IT, VIRTUALLY

Bitcoin and the rise of cryptocurrencies.

After the 2008 financial crash, confidence in the banking system was at an all-time low. Then, an anonymous person (or group of people) under the name Satoshi Nakamoto published a proposal that cryptography could be employed for financial transactions between individuals. Banks and major institutions would be cut out of the process entirely. The idea of bitcoin had been born: the first digital currency.

The viability of bitcoin hinges on the blockchain, a cryptographic tool that records transactions and details exactly who owns which coin. The system limits the total number of bitcoins to 21 million. In April 2018, the 17 millionth bitcoin was "mined", leaving only 4 million left to go. Its value has fluctuated wildly. When trading started on the first online bitcoin market it was worth less than 1 US cent. The first "bubble" saw its value reach $30, before plunging back to $2. Since then it has rocketed as the speculators piled in. On 17 December 2017, the value of one bitcoin reached just short of $20,000, although this wasn't sustained. Early adopters of bitcoin stood to make fortunes from its rise. Or perhaps in some cases lose a fortune. One IT worker from Newport in Wales had mistakenly thrown away a computer that contained 7,500 bitcoins in a digital wallet. At bitcoin's peak price, his lost laptop was worth almost $150 million.

Not everyone is a fan of bitcoin. Investor Warren Buffet, the renowned "sage of Omaha", described it in 2018 as "probably rat poison squared" and Jamie Dimon, CEO of JPMorgan Chase, labelled it a "fraud". It is also far from environmentally friendly: the energy usage of Bitcoin produces as much carbon dioxide per year as one million transatlantic flights.

The success of bitcoin has brought other cryptocurrencies into the market place: notably Litecoin (the second digital currency, described as "silver to bitcoin's gold"), Ethereum, Zcash, Dash and Monero.

In mid-August, 2018 one bitcoin was worth just over £5,000.

——————— TYRANNOSAURUS WRECKS: MASS EXTINCTIONS ———————

Scientists warn that we are now living through a sixth mass extinction event in the history of life on Earth, caused by overpopulation, environmental degradation and climate change. This is what happened during the previous five.

Late Ordovician, c.444 million years ago – glaciation and a fall in sea levels led to around 80% of all species dying out.

Late Devonian, c.360 million years ago – about three-quarters of all species became extinct during this period.

Permian –Triassic, 250 million years ago – known as The Great Dying, as around 95% of all marine and 70% of terrestrial species perished.

Late Triassic, 200 million years ago – accounted for the deaths of 75% of all species on Earth. It opened the way for dinosaurs to become the dominant land animals.

Cretaceous–Tertiary (K–T), 65 million years ago – the extinction event that witnessed the end of the dinosaurs and flying reptiles. The chief culprit is thought to be an asteroid that struck the Earth just off Mexico's Yucatán peninsula.

————————— PERCHANCE TO DREAM —————————

When we go to bed our sleep follows a 90-minute cycle of alternating REM (rapid eye movement) and NREM (non-rapid eye movement) sleep.

N1 (5% of sleep) – Transition from being awake to going to sleep. Muscle twitches known as "hypnic jerks" may occur.

N2 (50% of sleep) – Breathing and heart rate begin to slow. Body temperature falls.

N3 (20% of sleep) – The deepest stage of sleep. Sleep walking and talking takes place in this stage.

REM (25% of sleep) – Muscles relax and the eyes move back and forth. There is intense brain activity; most dreams occur during this stage.

REMEMBRANCE OF THINGS PASTA

It is an enduring myth that the traveller Marco Polo introduced pasta to Italy from China in the 13th century. The evidence suggests that Italians were enjoying pasta long before that. And it doesn't grow on trees either, as claimed in a celebrated April Fools' Day hoax on the TV programme *Panorama*. These are translations of many of the colourful and vivid names of common pasta types.

SHAPED

Castellane
(castle dwellers)

Farfalle
(butterflies)

Strozzapreti
(priest stranglers)

Conchiglie (shells)

Orecchiette
(little ears)

STRANDS

Barbina
(little beards)

Fedelini
(little faithful ones)

Vermicelli
(worms)

Capellini (fine hair)

Spaghetti
(little strings)

MINIATURE

Acini di pepe
(grains of pepper)

Occhi di pernice
(partridge eyes)

Stelle
(stars)

Ditali (thimbles)

Orzo (barley)

REMEMBRANCE OF THINGS PASTA

RIBBON

Fettuccine
(little slices)

Linguine
(little tongues)

Stringozzi
(shoe laces)

Lasagne
(cooking pot)

Reginette
(little queens)

SHORT EXTRUDED

Calamarata
(squid-like)

Fagioloni
(little beans)

Cavatappi
(corkscrews)

Penne (quills)

Fusilli (spindles)

FILLED

Cannelloni
(large reeds)

Fagottini
(little bundles)

Occhi di lupo
(wolf eyes)

Cappelletti (little hats)

Mezzelune (half moons)

SHATTERING THE GLASS CEILING

Women first!

1903   **Marie Curie** – first woman to win a Nobel Prize, for Physics. After winning again for Chemistry in 1911 she became the first person (and still the only woman) to receive two Nobel Prizes.

1915   **Edith Smith** – UK's first female police officer with powers of arrest. She patrolled the streets of Grantham during the First World War.

1918   **Constance Markievicz** – first woman elected to the House of Commons, although as a Sinn Fein member she did not take up her seat. Nancy Astor, in 1919, became the first woman to sit in the Commons.

1926   **Gertrude Ederle** – first woman to swim across the English Channel. Her time of 14 hours 39 minutes knocked almost two hours off the men's record.

1932   **Amelia Earhart** – first woman to fly solo across the Atlantic Ocean. She disappeared in the Pacific in 1937 while attempting to fly round the world.

1935   **Regina Jonas** – first woman to be ordained as a rabbi. She was murdered in Auschwitz in 1944.

1960   **Sirimavo Bandaranaike** – as prime minister of Sri Lanka, she was the world's first female head of government.

1963   **Valentina Tereshkova** – Soviet cosmonaut who became the first woman in space, orbiting the Earth in Vostok 6.

1975   **Junko Tabei** – Japanese mountaineer and the first woman to reach the summit of Mount Everest.

1979	**Margaret Thatcher** – first woman prime minister in Europe, staying in power in Britain until 1990.
1981	**Sandra Day O'Connor** – the first woman to serve on the US Supreme Court.
1984	**Svetlana Savitskaya** – first woman to perform a spacewalk, spending over three hours outside the Salyut 7 space station.
1994	**Angela Berners-Wilson** – first woman to be ordained as a Church of England priest.
1997	**Marjorie Scardino** – became the first female CEO of a FTSE 100 company when she took control of Pearson PLC.
2009	**Elinor Ostrom** – first and only woman to win the Nobel Prize in Economics.
2010	**Kathryn Bigelow** – first woman to win Best Director Oscar, for the Iraq War drama *The Hurt Locker*.
2013	**Marin Alsop** – first woman to conduct the Last Night of the Proms.

ROCKIN' A GOOD CAUSE

These are some of the biggest benefit gigs of the pop era.

Concert for Bangladesh, 1971 – Two concerts held in aid of refugees displaced by the Bangladesh War of Independence.

Live Aid, 1985 – Wembley Stadium in London and JFK in Philadelphia were the venues for the concerts to raise funds for famine relief in Ethiopia.

Freddie Mercury Tribute Concert, 1992 – A tribute to the late Queen singer with the aims of promoting AIDS awareness. Also held at Wembley.

Live 8, 2005 – Series of concerts in G8 countries and South Africa with the intention of encouraging aid and debt relief for developing countries.

---------------- **PUTTING PEDANTRY IN ITS PLACE** ----------------

When an overzealous editor altered Winston Churchill's copy so that a sentence didn't end in a preposition, the great man retorted "this is the kind of nonsense up with which I will not put". The story is probably fanciful but it neatly illustrates the point that many of the so-called "rules" of grammar can be safely ignored.

Sentences should not end with a preposition. They certainly can and this is nothing to fret over.

Sentences should not start with a conjunction. But they can. And they do.

Never split an infinitive. To slavishly adhere to this rule is foolish and can lead to clumsy writing. Captain Kirk got it right: "to boldly go" sounds much better than "boldly to go".

Doubles negatives are always wrong. Can't get no satisfaction? Don't need no education? I couldn't not point out these famous examples.

Avoid the passive. George Orwell can be blamed here. He emphasised an aversion to the passive in his writing advice in his essay "Politics and the English Language".

Singular "they" and "their" are always wrong. It was good enough for Geoffrey Chaucer in *The Canterbury Tales*: "And whoso fyndeth hym out of swich blame, They wol come up…" And *The King James Bible*: "So likewise shall my heavenly Father do also unto you, if ye from your hearts forgive not every one his brother their trespasses". And Shakespeare, too, in *The Comedy of Errors*: "There's not a man I meet but doth salute me, As if I were their well-acquainted friend".

---------------- **GOING ROUND IN CIRCLES 4** ----------------

The countries you pass through while travelling along some of the Earth's imaginary lines.

Tropic of Capricorn (East of the prime meridian)
Namibia • Botswana • South Africa • Mozambique • Madagascar •
Australia • Chile • Argentina • Paraguay • Brazil

———————— FROM PAYPAL TO PAYLOADS ————————

Elon Musk is a charismatic entrepreneur who has launched (sometimes literally) a series of ventures that have pushed the boundaries of technology.

PayPal – using the profits from his digital city guide business Zip2, Musk founded the online payment company X.com. This evolved into PayPal and although Musk left as CEO in 2000, its purchase by eBay ensured a windfall.

Tesla – Musk was a major early investor in the electric car company founded by Martin Eberhard and Marc Tarpenning. In 2008, its first car was introduced, the Roadster – a sports car that could travel 244 miles on a single charge and go from 0–60 mph in under four seconds.

SpaceX – Musk has long believed that humanity's future may depend on expanding beyond Earth. In 2002, he founded Space Exploration Technologies (SpaceX) to make reliable, reusable rockets. The first SpaceX rocket, Falcon 1, was launched in 2006 and the larger Falcon 9 followed four years later. In 2018, the world's most powerful rocket, Falcon Heavy, was launched from the Kennedy Space Center in Florida. It could carry a load of 64,000kg into orbit – more than twice as much as its nearest competitor, at a much cheaper cost. The payload for this test flight was Musk's old Tesla Roadster, with a dummy strapped in the driving seat, "Don't Panic" written on the dashboard and David Bowie playing on the stereo.

———————— UNFINISHED LITERARY BUSINESS ————————

The ink was still wet on these great works of literature when their authors died.

The Canterbury Tales	Geoffrey Chaucer
Don Juan	Lord Byron
Sanditon	Jane Austen
Wives and Daughters	Elizabeth Gaskell
The Mystery of Edwin Drood	Charles Dickens
The Pale King	David Foster Wallace

THERE'S NO "I" IN TEAM

How many players does it take to get a game going?

2 players	.. beach volleyball, ice dancing
3 players	... goalball, sepak takraw (Asian kick volleyball)
4 players	.... curling, polo, athletics and swimming relays
5 players	..... basketball
6 players	...... ice hockey, volleyball
7 players	.... netball, handball, kabaddi, rugby sevens, water polo
8 players	.... korfball, tug of war
9 players	.... baseball, rounders
10 players	.... men's lacrosse
11 players	.... football, cricket, hockey, American football
12 players	.... women's lacrosse, shinty, Canadian football
13 players	.... rugby league
15 players	.... rugby union, hurling, Gaelic football
16 players	.... elle (Sri Lankan baseball)
18 players	.... Australian rules football

COOKING WITH POO AND OTHER STRANGE TITLES

The Diagram Prize for the oddest book title of the year is awarded by the magazine *The Bookseller*. Here are some recent winners.

*The Commuter Pig Keeper: A Comprehensive Guide to
Keeping Pigs when Time is your Most Precious Commodity
Too Naked for the Nazis
Strangers have the Best Candy
How to Poo on a Date
Goblinproofing One's Chicken Coop
Cooking with Poo
Managing a Dental Practice: The Genghis Khan Way
The Stray Shopping Carts of Eastern North America:
A Guide to Field Identification
People Who Don't Know They're Dead: How They Attach
Themselves to Unsuspecting Bystanders and What to Do About It
Bombproof Your Horse*

──────────── LIVING LIFE ON THE EXTREMES ────────────

These are the places around the world where every day is a battle with the elements.

Hot – the hottest temperature reliably measured on Earth is 56.7°C (134.1°F) at the aptly named Furnace Creek Ranch in California's Death Valley in 1913. However, the record for the inhabited place with the highest average year-round temperature is Dallol in Ethiopia. Remote and arid, it lies in the Danakil Depression (nicknamed the "Gateway to Hell") at 130m below sea level.

Cold – the village of Oymyakon in Siberia is the coldest permanently inhabited place in the world. In 1933 it reached -68°C (-90°F), the lowest temperature recorded outside of Antarctica.

Wet – Mawsynram in north-eastern India has an average annual rainfall of nearly 12 metres. Most of it falls in the monsoon season between June and September.

Dry – in Chile's Atacama Desert some weather stations have never recorded rain. The city of Arica, on the Pacific coast of Chile, is often cited as the world's driest inhabited place by rainfall (or lack of it). However, this title is also claimed by the oasis of Quillagua, also in Chile, and the city of Aswan in southern Egypt.

──────────── FOOD, INGLORIOUS FOOD ────────────

Dishes from around the world that are guaranteed to make you lose your appetite.

Casu marzu, Italy – Sardinian "rotten cheese" that contains live maggots.
Escalemoles, Mexico – Ant larvae and pupae.
Shirako, Japan – Made from the sperm sacs of cod, angler fish and squid.
Tarantulas, Cambodia – Deep-fried giant spiders...mmm.
Century egg, China – Chicken, duck or quail eggs mixed into clay, ash, salt and quicklime.

—————————— **HOW MANY PLANETS ARE THERE?** ——————————

It's a simple-sounding question, but we can't make up our minds what the answer is.

Ancient times: 5 – Mercury, Venus, Mars, Jupiter and Saturn were known to the ancients. There was the Earth as well, of course, but in those days we thought the heavens revolved around us.

From 1543: 6 – Earth could be added to the list after the publication in 1543 of *On the Revolutions of the Celestial Spheres* by Nicolaus Copernicus. In it, he outlined his theory that the Sun, and not the Earth, was the centre of the planetary system.

From 1781: 7 – Uranus was discovered by the British astronomer William Herschel. He originally proposed naming it after George III.

From 1846: 8 – the existence of Neptune was predicted in the calculations of Urbain Le Verrier and confirmed by the observations of Johann Galle. It is the only giant planet not visible without a telescope.

From 1930: 9 – Pluto was discovered by Clyde Tombaugh in 1930 and recognised as the ninth planet of our solar system. Some of his ashes were on board the New Horizons probe that passed Pluto in 2015.

From 2006: 8 again – smaller than Earth's moon, Pluto was downgraded by the International Astronomical Union in 2006 to the new status of "dwarf planet". Four other bodies are currently recognised as dwarf planets: Ceres, Eris, Makemake and Haumea, although it is suspected there are around a hundred others in the solar system.

Are there any other planets out there? A hypothetical Planet Nine (or Planet X) has been proposed by astronomers, perhaps 10 times the size of Earth and 20 times further from the Sun than Neptune. Its existence would help explain the elliptical orbits of a group of objects in the distant Kuiper belt.

MENAGERIE OF MISNOMERS

Giraffes used to be known as camelopards because it was thought they had the head of a camel and the colouring of a leopard. Describing animals in terms of other animals can lead to confusion, as in the case of these creatures with misleading common names.

Firefly – also called glow worms, they are a family of beetles.

Koala bear – the arboreal Australian marsupial is not a bear of any description.

Slow worm – despite appearances, it is not a snake or worm but, in fact, a legless lizard.

Bearcat (binturong) – related to the civet, this Asian mammal is neither a bear nor a cat.

Horned toad – this name is given to a number of species of lizard found in North America. Their unusual defence mechanism is the ability to squirt blood from the corner of their eyes.

Starfish – not fish but echinoderms of the class Asteroidea. There are over 1,500 species of starfish.

Velvet ant – any of around 3,000 species of wasp. They get their name from the resemblance of the wingless females to ants.

PARK AND RIDE

These are the world's most popular amusement parks.

Rank	Park	Attendees (2016)
1	Magic Kingdom, Walt Disney World, Florida	20,395,000
2	Disneyland, California	17,943,000
3	Tokyo Disneyland, Tokyo	16,540,000
4	Universal Studio Japan, Osaka	14,500,000
5	Tokyo Disney Sea, Tokyo	13,460.000

─────── METRIC/IMPERIAL CONVERSIONS ───────

LENGTH

From Imperial	Multiply by	From Metric	Multiply by
inches to cm	2.54	cm to inches	0.393701
feet to metres	0.3048	metres to feet	3.28084
yards to m	0.9144	m to yards	1.09361
miles to km	1.609344	km to miles	0.621371

AREA

From Imperial	Multiply by	From Metric	Multiply by
inches^2 to cm^2	6.4516	cm^2 to inches^2	0.155
feet^2 to m^2	0.092903	m^2 to feet^2	10.7639
yards^2 to m^2	0.836127	m^2 to yards^2	1.19599
miles^2 to km^2	2.589988	km^2 to niles^2	0.386102

VOLUME

From Imperial	Multiply by	From Metric	Multiply by
cubic inches to cubic cm	16.387064	cubic cm to cubic inches	0.061024
cubic feet to cubic metres	0.028317	cubic metres to cubic feet	35.3147
pints to litres	0.568261	litres to pints	1.759754

MASS

From Imperial	Multiply by	From Metric	Multiply by
ounces to g	28.349523	g to ounces	0.035274
pounds to kg	0.453592	kg to pounds	2.20462
stones to kg	6.350293	kg to stones	0.157473

FROM ONE DAY TO THE NEXT

The number of days from any day in a particular month to the same day in another. How many days are there from 1st November to 1st July? Find November in the first column and July in the head of the table and that is the number of days required. But if the given days are different, then add or subtract the difference: for instance, for 1st November to 10th July, add nine days to the number found in the table; and for 10th November to 1st July subtract nine days. Add one if it's a leap year and 29 February falls between the days in question.

	Jan.	Feb.	Mar.	Apr.	May	June	July	Aug.	Sep.	Oct.	Nov.	Dec.
Jan.	365	31	59	90	120	151	181	212	243	273	304	334
Feb.	334	365	28	59	89	120	150	181	212	242	273	303
Mar.	306	337	365	31	61	92	122	153	184	214	245	275
Apr.	275	306	334	365	30	61	91	122	153	183	214	244
May	245	276	304	335	365	31	61	92	123	153	184	214
June	214	245	273	304	334	365	30	61	92	122	153	183
July	184	215	243	274	304	335	365	31	62	92	123	153
Aug.	153	184	212	243	273	304	334	365	31	61	92	122
Sep.	122	153	181	212	242	273	303	334	365	30	61	91
Oct.	92	123	151	182	212	243	273	304	334	365	31	61
Nov.	61	92	120	151	181	212	242	273	304	334	365	30
Dec.	31	62	90	121	151	182	212	243	274	304	335	365

——— HOW DO YOU LIKE THEM APPS? ———

It is predicted that in 2018 over 200 billion apps will be downloaded by the world's smartphone users. Android users have a choice of 3.8 million apps on Google Play, while Apple offers over 2 million to choose from at the App Store. These are not the only places to get an app, of course, but the dominance of the two big marketplaces suggests a duopoly. At the Worldwide Developers Conference in 2018, Apple CEO Tim Cook said that in the ten years of the App Store the company had paid out $100 billion to iOS software developers. Currently there are 20 million Apple developers across the world, trying to come up with the next big thing for the 1.3 billion active devices in use (iPhones, Macs, iPads, iPods, Apple TVs and Apple Watches).

In 2017, the top ten App Store downloads were:

1. Bitmoji
2. Snapchat
3. YouTube
4. Messenger
5. Instagram
6. Facebook
7. Google Maps
8. Netflix
9. Spotify
10. Uber

——— SPACE ODDITIES ———

Since the dawn of the space age there have been around 5,400 successful rocket launches. That's left an awful lot of junk up there.

8,650 satellites of all sizes have been launched since Sputnik in 1957. Around 4,700 of these are still in space and, as of 2018, about 1,800 are still functioning. Approximately 21,000 items of space debris have been tracked and catalogued by the Space Surveillance Networks. The total mass of these objects in Earth orbit is more than 8,100 tonnes.

The estimated breakdown of space junk is 29,000 objects larger than 10cm; 750,000 objects from 1cm to 10cm; 166 million objects from 1mm to 1cm.

NEWS (CENSORED)

The independence of the media is under attack across the world. Each year the organisation Reporters Without Borders compiles an index ranking press freedom in every country in the world (the higher the rank, the greater the freedom of the press. These are where some prominent nations are placed.

1. Norway	87. Israel
2. Sweden	102. Brazil
3. Netherlands	138. India
4. Finland	148. Russia
5. Switzerland	157. Turkey
15. Germany	164. Iran
18. Canada	176. China
19. Australia	177. Syria
40. UK	178. Turkmenistan
45. USA	179. Eritrea
67. Japan	180. North Korea

GIVE 'EM ENOUGH ROPE

Capital punishment is on the wane across the world.

The last hanging took place in Britain in 1964. In France, the guillotine was used as recently as 1977. Now, Belarus is the only country in Europe that still uses the death penalty.

In 2017, Amnesty International recorded at least 993 executions in 23 different countries. This figure excludes China, where an estimated 2,000 executions took place; the exact number is a closely-guarded state secret. After China, the death penalty was most used in Iran, Saudi Arabia, Iraq and Pakistan. Those four countries alone accounted for 84% of the total recorded by Amnesty. Other states carrying out executions included Egypt, Bahrain, Jordan, Kuwait, the United Arab Emirates, Palestine, Singapore, Somalia and South Sudan. The USA is the only country in the Americas to use the death penalty, executing 23 people in 2017.

———————— **SELECTED SOURCES** ————————

Archaeological Institute of America
American National Biography
Atlas Obscura
Bartleby.com
BBC News
BBC Sport
Billboard
British Library
British Museum
BUPA
CIA World Factbook
CNN
Credo Reference
The Daily Mail
The Daily Telegraph
The Economist
Encyclopaedia Britannica
European Union
Facebook
Field Studies Council
FIFA
Flags of the World
Google
The Guardian
Guinness World Records
HBO
The Independent
Instagram
International Olympic Committee
International Union for Conservation of Nature
King James Bible
London Mayor's office
London Review of Books
Marvel Comics
Met Office
Metropolitan Transportation Authority
NASA
The National Archives

National Geographic
Nature
Newsweek
Oxford Art online
Oxford Companion to English Literature
Oxford Companion to Military History
Oxford Dictionary of Astronomy
Oxford Dictionary of Environment and Conservation
Oxford Dictionary of Biology
Oxford Dictionary of National Biography
Oxford Dictionary of Quotations
Oxford English Dictionary
Oxford Music online
Oxford Reference online
People
Project Gutenberg
Radio Times
Royal Family website
Royal Society of Chemistry
RSPB
Science Museum
Smithsonian Institution
Statista
Tate
Time
The Times
Toy Retailers Association
Transport for London
Twitter
UK Parliament
UNESCO
United Nations
US Environmental Protection Agency
US Library of Congress
Variety
White House
Wired
Woodland Trust
WWF
Zoological Society of London

"In this life, we want nothing but Facts, sir; nothing but Facts!"

– Mr. Gradgrind, *Hard Times* by Charles Dickens